MADEMOISELLE COLOMBE

MADEMOISELLE COLOMBE

A play by
JEAN ANOUILH

Adapted by
LOUIS KRONENBERGER

Coward-McCann, Inc.

New York

To Sylvia and Seymour Peck
with the adapter's affection

Mademoiselle Colombe opened at the Longacre Theatre in New York City on January 6, 1954. It was produced by Robert L. Joseph and Jay Julien and was directed by Harold Clurman. The production was designed by Boris Aronson with costumes by Motley. The cast, in order of appearance, was as follows:

COLOMBE	*Julie Harris*
JULIEN	*Eli Wallach*
MME. GEORGES	*Edna Preston*
MME. ALEXANDRA	*Edna Best*
CHIROPODIST	*Edward Julien*
MANICURIST	*Joanne Taylor*
HAIRDRESSER	*Nehemiah Persoff*
GOURETTE	*Sam Jaffe*
EDOUARD	*William Windom*
DESCHAMPS	*Frank Silvera*
POET-MINE-OWN	*Mikhail Rasumny*
GAULOIS	*Harry Bannister*
DANCERS	{ *Lee Phillips* { *Jeanne Jerrems*
STAGEHAND	*Gregory Robins*

MADEMOISELLE COLOMBE

A THEATRE IN PARIS

ACT I Scene 1

SCENE: *The corridor flanking the dressing rooms, with one whole side of Mme. Alexandra's dressing room exposed, and at one end the door to her inner retiring room. The corridor is badly lighted; the dressing room is still dark.*

AT RISE: COLOMBE *is seated and* JULIEN *pacing back and forth. They seem to be waiting for something. The dresser,* MME. GEORGES, *comes in carrying a chair.*

MME. GEORGES:
Sit down, Mr. Julien. You'll probably have to wait a while.

JULIEN:
> *At some distance.*

Thanks, Georgie—but I just told you I'd rather stand.

MME. GEORGES:
My oldest boy had to stand, too. Now he's got varicose veins. I always have to sit and it's just the opposite— my rear end hurts.

JULIEN:
Oh, go bury your rear end. I wish the old girl would hurry up.

3

MME. GEORGES:
> *To* COLOMBE.

It starts with an itch in the feet, then it goes into the legs, then it gets you in the back. . . .

JULIEN:
> *Shouting to* COLOMBE.

For God's sake, tell her you're not interested. If you don't, she'll show you over her whole body.

MME. GEORGES:
Thirty years I've been a dresser, Mrs. Julien, always sitting around waiting for the play to end.

COLOMBE:
But you don't *have* to sit.

MME. GEORGES:
Yes I do. My phlebitis.

JULIEN:
The hell with your phlebitis. Find out if the old girl's on stage.

MME. GEORGES:
> *Shaking her head.*

Uh-uhm. She always goes to her dressing room before she rehearses.—A fine way to refer to your mother.

JULIEN:
Stop lecturing me.

4

MME. GEORGES:

Listen to him. My oldest all over again. I will say, my third one, the one who died of T.B., he was easy to bring up—always spitting quietly in his corner.

To COLOMBE:

How old is *your* baby?

COLOMBE:

Just a year.

MME. GEORGES:

Are his movements regular?

JULIEN:

Grabbing her in exasperation by the arm.

Georgie, if you don't shut up, I'll break your neck.

MME. GEORGES:

Quite unruffled.

Men, Mrs. Julien.—I've known him since he was so high.

JULIEN:

Uhm. That's how long I've been hearing all this.

MME. GEORGES:

He was a *nice* little boy. Used to ask for caramels. Didn't you?

JULIEN:

Letting her go and walking off.

If you say so.

MME. GEORGES:
>> *To* JULIEN.

You didn't have strong lungs either.

JULIEN:

They're much stronger now. The caramels cured me.

MME. GEORGES:
>> *Sudden thought.*

I hope the baby doesn't cough?

JULIEN:

Georgie, my son doesn't cough, my wife doesn't cough,
>> *Indicating himself.*

none of us cough.—Go on,
>> *Indicating downstairs.*

see if she hasn't come.

MME. GEORGES:
>> *Impervious.*

My fourth son, the one in the Foreign Legion, developed a sort of a dog bark.

JULIEN:

Georgie, you *sure* they're rehearsing today? I've got to see her.

MME. GEORGES:

Gets married without a word, waits two years, and then calmly strolls in just before a rehearsal.
>> *To* JULIEN.

Don't worry, you'll see her—and hear from her, too. You and your mother have never gotten along. Not like Mr. Édouard: he knows how to handle her.

JULIEN:

What's she playing in now?

MME. GEORGES:

The Goddess of Love. A play with five changes. Why can't she do *Athalie* again—a classic, and she only has to change once.

JULIEN:

Georgie, it's damn near three o'clock. Be a good girl, go down and see if the others haven't come.

MME. GEORGES:

> *Exiting as though her aches and pains were pieces of heavy luggage.*

Two flights of stairs: have you any idea how many times I go up and down every day?
> *Exit.*

JULIEN:

The Goddess of Love. One of her *femme fatale* roles. That's bad.

COLOMBE:

Why?

JULIEN:

The only times I've made even a dent on her were

7

when she was cast as a mother. The theatre's sure something!

COLOMBE:

You make too much of everything.

JULIEN:

Do I?

Eruptively.

When I was four, the Mater sent me to live with a blacksmith twenty miles outside Paris. For months she never came near me. Just as I was half dead from cold and hunger, Poet-Mine-Own brought her the script of *The Sins of the Mother*. In the first act she abandons her baby on the steps of a church—snowing outside, singing within. In the fifth act she's stabbed with remorse for 91 lines. I once counted them.—After the dress rehearsal, she got into a carriage with two friends and a photographer to see the poor little kid it broke her heart to have to board out. Imagine the publicity: Mme. Alexandra, the nation's greatest emotional actress, who every night abandons her baby in the theatre, photographed in real life with a little four-year-old she adores. Except that the four-year-old was such a mass of skin and bones, and so scabby with dirt, they couldn't photograph him.—The next night Mommy had all Paris drenched in tears. The rumor had spread that with her own child at death's door, she'd insisted on going on. The play was a smash. At least I got *something* out of

8

it—she sent me to live in Switzerland like a human being.

COLOMBE:
My poor Julien. I never realized. . . .

JULIEN:
I've never run down
With a sarcastic inflection.
literature since. Thanks to Poet-Mine-Own's throbbing verses, I'm well enough today to serve in the army.

COLOMBE:
Is Poet-Mine-Own . . . ?

JULIEN:
Yes. Robinet. He calls Mommy "Madame Inspiration" and she calls him "Poet-Mine-Own." You'll get used to it!

COLOMBE:
After a brief pause.
Do you think she'll do anything for us?

JULIEN:
Not if she can help it. But I don't see how she can—a soldier son and his gallant little wife. She'll have to do something.

COLOMBE:
It's not nice to talk that way.

9

JULIEN:

I know. Don't you think I'd like the word "mother" to stand for something . . . good?

COLOMBE:

Why is she so fond of your brother?

JULIEN:

To begin with, Edouard's jockey father was the one real love of her life. She still sends him money. Edouard learned fast how to get on in the world—he'd hang around the theatre getting hugged and kissed, a little angel sucking a lollipop. I remind the old girl of my father—a moody army officer.

COLOMBE:

Darling, you aren't always easy to live with, you know. Either you're yelling your head off about something or you refuse to open your mouth. Was your father that way, too?

JULIEN:

Apparently he was considered impossible. So honest himself that he made everyone else squirm. And like a first-class misanthrope, he carefully fell in love with a woman who could only break his heart. He thought mother would make him sublimely happy. She did, for three weeks. Then she left him for the juvenile lead.

COLOMBE:

And your father killed himself?

JULIEN:
Yes.

COLOMBE:
How ghastly!

JULIEN:
Yes. Mother was terribly put out.

COLOMBE:
Julien, she's still your mother. Don't you think if you tried a little harder ... ?

JULIEN:
No, my love, I don't.

COLOMBE:
I'm afraid you're impossible, too.

JULIEN:
"Impossible" is an unpatriotic word—don't you dare apply it to a prospective soldier of France.

COLOMBE:
If you'd ask your mother, I'm sure with the people she knows you could be deferred.

JULIEN:
No thanks. I hate it, but I'll go through with it.

COLOMBE:

Just because you hate it?
He smiles faintly.
And what about me all that time?

JULIEN:

Going to her, suddenly gentle.
Darling, you're all I've got. It's going to be hell to leave you—but you wouldn't love me if I walked out on the job to stay with you.

COLOMBE:

Are you crazy? Of course I'd love you.

JULIEN:

Well, I can't. You might love me, but I'd only hate myself.

COLOMBE:

With a sigh.
You make everything a problem.
MME. GEORGES *rushes in, talking loudly.*

MME. GEORGES:

She's here! She's downstairs, giving some students her autograph.

JULIEN:

Haven't they unhitched her carriage horses and put themselves between the shafts? Aren't they imploring her to let 'em pull her through the streets?

MME. GEORGES:

If you're going to start in that way...
Sympathetically.
Don't, Mr. Julien. When I see what your brother
manages to get with a little flattery...

JULIEN:

Georgie, you just feel sorry for *yourself*. I'll handle me.

MME. GEORGES:

After shaking her head at COLOMBE.
Anyway, I'm going to let her know you're here.
Exit.

COLOMBE:

Going up to JULIEN.
Darling, you know what we're here for. Please be
nice. Think of the baby...and me.

JULIEN:

Pricking his ears.
Listen to that—just listen to that. It puffs, it pants, it
wheezes, it yanks its damn carcass up step by step—
who'd ever believe that on stage it's a young girl, it's
youth itself—it doesn't even walk, it floats. That's my
mother!

COLOMBE:

Shouting in protest.
Julien!

JULIEN:

Stand at attention! Before you shall appear the goddess of love of the entire Third Republic.—I know you go for love; you'll be impressed.

COLOMBE:

Darling, I'm frightened.

JULIEN:

Oh, it doesn't bite.

COLOMBE:

Julien, it's you I'm frightened of.

> MME. ALEXANDRA *appears, surrounded by* MME. GEORGES *and a collection of hairdressers, chiropodists, etc. Sweeps past* COLOMBE *and* JULIEN *without so much as a look, and bangs into her dressing room.*

MME. ALEXANDRA:

> *Snappish.*

My son! Of course not. Tell him I don't care to see him.

> *The dressing room door is shut.*

JULIEN:

> *Sits like a stone, aghast, till his mother disappears. Then bursts out.*

This is just a little too much! This time I'll show her!

COLOMBE:

> *Trying to restrain him.*

My darling, calm down. You won't get anywhere by yelling.

JULIEN:

Let me go. I feel like yelling. I'd choke if I didn't. Mother!

> *He flings himself upon her dressing room, knocks at the inner dressing room door, which is locked. Rattles it.*

Mother! Let me in! Let me in, or I'll break the door down.

> *Rattles on in vain.*

Mme. Alexandra, if you don't open the door, I'll smash all your imitation china, I'll rip up your fake Persian rugs. Let me in, or it'll cost you a damn sight more than anything I want from you.

> *The dressing room door opens a little. The* CHIROPODIST *appears, clutching it firmly.*

CHIROPODIST:

Madame wishes to inform monsieur that she can't see him. She has a rehearsal.

JULIEN:

> *Through the half-open door.*

Mme. Alexandra, I am calm. I am inconceivably, indescribably calm. But this just happens to be something that I can't go into with your chiropodist.

MME. ALEXANDRA:

> *From within.*

Tell him to get out of my dressing room and wait in the corridor.

JULIEN:

> *Teeth clenched, white with anger; suddenly.*

As you wish, mummy dear. I'll wait in the corridor, mummy dear.

> *He goes out, slamming the door; turns red when he sees* COLOMBE *trembling.*

Was I calm enough for you?

> *The* CHIROPODIST *closes the door and waits there till* MME. GEORGES *goes out and through the corridor to lock it again—a sneaky, self-important bit of pantomime.*

MME. GEORGES:

You sure are making headway, Mr. Julien. I begged you to behave.

JULIEN:

Sorry. Frightfully sorry.

MME. GEORGES:

After all, it's you that wants the help—you're the one that's got to make the effort.

JULIEN:

Did I walk past *her?* Did I refuse to see *her?*

MME. GEORGES:
> *After a second.*

How much do you want? Maybe if she knew the amount...

JULIEN:

I have to serve my country. I want her to look after my wife and child while I'm away.

MME. GEORGES:
> *With a low whistle.*

Three years is a long time.

JULIEN:
> *Significantly.*

Yes.

> *During all this,* MME. ALEXANDRA *has changed into a dressing gown. She sits on a kind of throne: the* CHIROPODIST *takes her foot, the* MANICURIST *her hand, the* HAIR-DRESSER *her head.* GOURETTE, *her secretary, stands waiting, papers in hand. There is the sense of an ancient idol companied by priests.*

MME. ALEXANDRA:
> *After a moment.*

Gourette!

GOURETTE:
> *Advancing obsequiously.*

Yes, madame?

MME. ALEXANDRA:
What's the mail?

GOURETTE:
A bill for your *Goddess of Love* costumes. It's the
third one.

MME. ALEXANDRA:
Really? What else?

GOURETTE:
The stagehands want a raise.

MME. ALEXANDRA:
They do? What else?

GOURETTE:
The Consumptive Students Aid Society are having a
benefit.

MME. ALEXANDRA:
I've already given the students.

GOURETTE:
These are consumptive students.

MME. ALEXANDRA:
Are they students or are they consumptives?

GOURETTE:
They say that Mme. Sarah Bernhardt sent them a
statue she carved herself.

MME. ALEXANDRA:

Tell them I'm not a sculptress, like Mme. Sarah Bern-hardt—I merely act.

GOURETTE:

Mme. Sarah Bernhardt's gift will get a lot of publicity.

MME. ALEXANDRA:

Anything Mme. Sarah Bernhardt does gets a lot of publicity. Is it a big statue?

GOURETTE:

If it's the one she exhibited at the last Salon, it's about this big.

MME. ALEXANDRA:

Is that all? I'm amazed.
                    Calls out.

Georges!

MME. GEORGES:

            In the corridor, to JULIEN.
She wants me. You stay here now—it'll work out all right.

            She goes into the dressing room with her
            passkey, closing the door behind her.
Yes, madame?

MME. ALEXANDRA:

What did you do with that great big bronze horror— that thing I never could get rid of?

MME. GEORGES:
The naked lady?

MME. ALEXANDRA:
The naked lady's a Rodin! Give them a Rodin just because they've got consumption?

MME. GEORGES:
Oh—you don't mean the Skeleton?

MME. ALEXANDRA:
Tha-a-at's it. Skeleton pulling someone after him.

MME. GEORGES:
It's called "Death and the Young Man."—It's at home—in the attic.

MME. ALEXANDRA:
To GOURETTE.
Send it with my very best wishes.

GOURETTE:
But "Death and the Young Man"—for young men with consumption?

MME. ALEXANDRA:
And why not? It's one of the *few* things that'll make them feel how well off they are.

JULIEN:
Impatient.
If she thinks she can keep me waiting all afternoon ...

COLOMBE:
Please, Julien, I beg of you.

JULIEN:
Goes and knocks at the door.
Mother!
The whole dressing room stops dead, waiting for MME. ALEXANDRA'S *next move.*

MME. ALEXANDRA:
To GOURETTE.
What else?

JULIEN:
Knocking again.
Mother!

GOURETTE:
A young man from Rouen who's seen you three times in *The Goddess of Love* and would die for you.

MME. ALEXANDRA:
Good. Thank him. What else?

JULIEN:
Knocking.
Mother! Let me in.
The dressing room stops dead again.

MME. ALEXANDRA:
To GOURETTE.
What else?

GOURETTE:

> *Dead pan.*

A line from Mr. Julien, that he's coming here to see you today on very urgent business.

MME. ALEXANDRA:

What else?

JULIEN:

> *Kicking the door.*

Mother! I'll keep kicking the door till you let me in.

MME. ALEXANDRA:

> *To* GOURETTE, *who has been listening, with a faint smile, to* JULIEN.

Did you hear me? I asked, what else?

GOURETTE:

> *The smile vanishing.*

The firemen, madame.

MME. ALEXANDRA:

What can they want? There's no fire.

GOURETTE:

Their annual benefit...

JULIEN:

> *Who has gone on kicking the door.*

Mother! Mme. Alexandra! If you don't give a damn about me, think of the beautiful paint on the door.

COLOMBE:

Dragging him away.
Julien, that's enough—you're being dreadful!

JULIEN:

Stops; looks at her; quietly.
Oh—you think I'm awful, too? All right, I'll stop.
Goes and sits down.

MME. ALEXANDRA:
What else?

GOURETTE:
What shall I do about the firemen?

MME. ALEXANDRA:
Oh—send them all the flowers that came yesterday.

GOURETTE:
Flowers, to firemen?

MME. ALEXANDRA:
Certainly.

GOURETTE:
But they're really rather faded.

MME. ALEXANDRA:
They can water them. Watering things is their spe-
cialty.
Gets up.
That's enough for now. I'm tired. I'm going to get
ready for rehearsal.

23

GOURETTE:

As you wish, madame.

> *Exits:* MME. GEORGES *goes to open the door for him with her passkey, motions to* JULIEN *and* COLOMBE *to wait quietly.* MME. ALEXANDRA *goes into her inner dressing room followed by her staff;* MME. GEORGES *quickly rejoins her. Alone in the corridor with* JULIEN *and* COLOMBE, GOURETTE *changes his tone.*

GOURETTE:

The bitch!

JULIEN:

> *Looking at him.*

Yes.

GOURETTE:

> *Coming closer.*

It's been like that every day for ten years. "Yes, Mme. Alexandra." "Quite, Mme. Alexandra." "Oh, at once, Mme. Alexandra."

> *Suddenly, after a cowardly glance at the closed dressing room door.*

God damn your stinking soul, Mme. Alexandra! ... When will I be able to say it to her face?

JULIEN:

Any time you care to. You're a free agent.

24

GOURETTE:

You can say that; you're her son. Mama's boy can act up now and then. But mama's secretary: he either says nothing or he says, "Indeed yes, Mme. Alexandra" —and with a smile, too. That's part of the contract. —Sometimes, if I don't guess right off exactly what she wants, know how she tells me? Heaves a statuette at my face. By now, I've learned to duck—but even then, I have to keep on smiling. What temperament!—she *couldn't* be anything but a genius. We admire her, God how we admire her, God how sick we are of admiring her. It's a privilege to serve her—it has to be, it's such a damn lousy living.

JULIEN:

Why do you stay?

GOURETTE:

Because I need my . . . two meals a day. They're all I do need, with everything else I have to swallow. "Why do I stay?" Why do you suppose I stay? Why do you come? . . . If just once I had the guts to . . .

JULIEN:

Get out of here. You're disgusting.

GOURETTE:

Yes, I know. I'm disgusting, I'm nauseating, I'm a worm, I'm anything you care to call me. But don't worry—someday the worm will turn.—Run along now, kiss mommy like a good boy. We all have our pride, we all have our principles, we all can be pushed just so far—only next thing you know, we're bowing right down to the ground.

> *He exits with a nasty laugh.* JULIEN *remains standing, distraught.*

JULIEN:

> *Suddenly.*

I'm sick—let's get out of here.

> *At this moment* EDOUARD *appears, walking rapidly toward the dressing room. Stops, amazed, in front of* JULIEN.

EDOUARD:

My God—Julien! Where'd you come from?

> *Notices* COLOMBE.

And who's the young lady?

JULIEN:

My wife. My brother Edouard.

EDOUARD:

Oh, of course: I'd forgotten. . . . Where in God's name have you two been—two years and not even a postcard. Were you in America?

JULIEN:

I was in Belleville, giving piano lessons. And Belleville's not exactly a music center.

26

EDOUARD:

And now you've come to kiss and make up—
Smiles.
Want help?

JULIEN:

No thanks. We're leaving.

EDOUARD:

Come on, let me have a shot at it. I'll make it easy for you.

JULIEN:

Thanks; you're very kind, but we're leaving.

EDOUARD:

Need anything? I'm flat myself, from the horses. But
Indicating the dressing room.
help is at hand—a mere matter of minutes. Hold on, don't move.

JULIEN:

No. We were in the neighborhood, so we thought we'd call. Madame's not at home. Don't worry, it doesn't matter. And it was nice to see you.
Tries to stop COLOMBE *from going to* ED-OUARD.

COLOMBE:

Don't listen to Julien, monsieur. He's so ... proud. He did come to try to see your mother.

JULIEN:
> *Trying to shut her up.*

Quit it, Colombe.

COLOMBE:

We have a little baby, and Julien's about to go in the army. We came to ask his mother to look after us while he's gone.

EDOUARD:
> *Incredulous.*

You didn't ask to be deferred?

JULIEN:

No. I leave for camp tomorrow.

EDOUARD:

And this child stays behind, flat broke and with a baby in her arms? That's what you're here to explain?

COLOMBE:

Exactly, monsieur. And because his mother couldn't see us right away, he insists on leaving.

EDOUARD:

I must say, you haven't changed any.
> *To* COLOMBE.

He's going to make you extremely unhappy, my child.

COLOMBE:

I love him, monsieur.

EDOUARD:

I'm sure you do. We all love him. But that needn't stop us from thinking that life isn't quite the torture chamber he makes it.—And if I hadn't come along, he was going to march off straight to camp and save France?—First of all, my hero, we're going to get you deferred.

COLOMBE:

Julien, you see!

JULIEN:

No, thank you. I don't want to be deferred.

EDOUARD:

Of course not! You prefer "left, right, left" with sixty pounds of assorted lead and iron on your back. —I don't blame you—it sounds fascinating. And what fun for this charming young lady—she can be all alone in Belleville, washing diapers or trying to find the money for the baby's milk. One can be a patriot, you know, without making one's wife join the breadline! Please, wait five minutes—let me see what I can do.

> *Goes into the dressing room, enters the inner retiring room without knocking, calls out gaily.*

Mother darling, I bid you good day!

> JULIEN *doesn't move:* COLOMBE, *with an admiring look at the departing* EDOUARD, *comes closer to* JULIEN.

COLOMBE:

My, he's nice. See, I was right to tell him about us.

JULIEN:

Yes.

Suddenly, in a different voice.

Colombe—listen to me. After tomorrow, you'll be alone here—and life's not quite everything you think it is.

COLOMBE:

I know, my darling.

JULIEN:

It can be very tough. It has nothing to do with the pretty speeches people make.

COLOMBE:

I know. You've told me before.

JULIEN:

Now you'll find out for yourself. All the things that impress you about . . .

Slight gesture toward dressing room.

. . . these people, are just for show.

COLOMBE:

Yes, Julien.

JULIEN:

I know how good your intentions are: but you're still just a child, you can't know what goes with their idea of a good time—or what comes after.

30

COLOMBE:

Laughing a little.
I ought to be scared to death?

JULIEN:

There's nothing to laugh at.—Yes, you ought to be scared to death.

COLOMBE:

Darling, I'll really try to be, if that pleases you. But is "their idea of a good time" really so awful?

JULIEN:

Yes.

COLOMBE:

Things like someone telling me I'm beautiful and wanting to buy me flowers?

JULIEN:

Yes.

COLOMBE:

But what can be the harm if I say "thank you" for the flowers, and that's the end of it? It doesn't mean a thing—it's you I love.

JULIEN:

I know. But it's not going to be simple. I'll be way off somewhere—if you really love me...

COLOMBE:

Darling, I do love you—no one but you.

31

JULIEN:

You don't know how I want to believe you.—Are you listening?—you're not looking at me.

COLOMBE:

I'm not looking at you, but I'm listening—very hard.

JULIEN:

His seriousness slightly comic.

If you love me as you say you do, you'll forget about such things.

COLOMBE:

With a tender little smile: incredulously.

No pretty things or corsages—or even compliments? I can't look around in shops at all the beautiful clothes I can't afford?

JULIEN:

Unhappily.

No, baby.

COLOMBE:

But I don't want you to buy them for me. I just want to look at them. What harm can it do to look at them?

JULIEN:

I don't even want you to look at them.

COLOMBE:

You're asking something awfully difficult.

32

JULIEN:

Everything good is difficult.

COLOMBE:

I'd know what you meant if you said I mustn't let anyone else buy them for me; but . . .

JULIEN:

No, Colombe. Try to see what I mean. You're my wife: when you married me, you were willing to get along with what I could give you; you were willing— weren't you?—to be poor.

COLOMBE:

Yes.

JULIEN:

I warned you what it would mean—babies keeping us awake at night, your hands all red from washing dishes. You didn't have to agree to it—and yet you did.

COLOMBE:

I did because I loved you.

JULIEN:

I know. But it's not enough to love me. I won't be here. Promise as the two of us did. . . .

COLOMBE:

You mean before that awful mayor with his break- fast in his beard? That time doesn't count.

33

JULIEN:

Then promise, as we promised the priest.

COLOMBE:

All right, I promise. Now are you happy?

JULIEN:

Cross your heart.

COLOMBE:

Cross my heart. But it's not because I promise, silly—
it's because I love you.

JULIEN:

No. Don't you see: that's not it. Tomorrow maybe you
won't love me. I want it to be because we chose each
other, because we've become part of each other.

COLOMBE:

Half mystified, half hurt.
Then it doesn't even matter that I love you?

JULIEN:

Of course it matters, but I mean something more.
Look. Please. I could have known somebody else, you
could have known somebody else, and loved him for
his looks or something. That kind of love we can feel
for lots of people, because we're young and need love.
You're something different. Other people are hard or
mean, and the ones that aren't bastards are blockheads.
Ever since I was a little kid all they've done is hurt
me. I hate them.

34

COLOMBE:

You don't go out of your way to make friends yourself.

JULIEN:

Not that kind of friends. I've built a better world of my own. A world that means you, and that little monkey that just grins at us, before he really lets us know what he's like.

COLOMBE:

He's your son, whatever he's like. If he's not everything you want when he grows up, won't you love him anyhow?

JULIEN:

With a fierce sincerity.

No.

COLOMBE:

Then you only love us for our good points: if I lied or stole or something, you wouldn't love me?

JULIEN:

I don't know.

COLOMBE:

Do you think that means a *thing?* You've got to love me faults and all.

JULIEN:

You've only got a few little-girl's faults.

COLOMBE:

And if someday I had a great many big-girl's faults—
bad faults—then you wouldn't love me?—And you
think that's love?

JULIEN:

Yes.

COLOMBE:

Yes—you do. But that's not how I want to be loved.
I want you to love me as a woman, not as a little girl.

JULIEN:

Smiling; beaten.

All right, when I get out of the army, I promise I'll
love you that way. We'll throw the most god-awful
scenes, we'll stage the most terrific reconciliations. But
while I'm away, darling, do what I ask: keep away
from these people.

Suddenly, at once comic and touching.

Be the way I like you to be.

COLOMBE:

Still a little irritated.

I always am—you should know that.

JULIEN:

Hesitates: then bursts out.

He'll be back! Another thing, Colombe—don't start
seeing much of Edouard.

COLOMBE:

But he's so nice.

36

JULIEN:

> *Savagely.*

You mustn't just because he's so nice. If you love me, you won't—because I'm not nice.

COLOMBE:

Is that something to brag about? It's nice to be nice.

JULIEN:

No!

COLOMBE:

> *With a comic little sigh.*

Darling, how complicated you make everything! How careful I keep having to be. And it's really so simple— people are nice, if you're nice to them.

EDOUARD:

> *Coming back, shouts.*

Still there, you lovebirds?

> *Comes into the corridor, looking pleased.*

One for our side, children! She refuses to see the undutiful son but is all agog to meet his wife. Incidentally —what name shall I say?

COLOMBE:

> *Like a schoolgirl.*

Colombe, monsieur.

EDOUARD:

I *like* it—but what *is* it?

COLOMBE:

A saint's name.

EDOUARD:

That's too bad. But I'm sure she wasn't a ... terribly
saintly saint. Took Thursdays off, or something.

To JULIEN.

Sonny, stay put for just five minutes: if Ma sees you
now, she'll hit the ceiling. First let's have her warm
up to Colombe, then you come on in the second act.
You know the scene: the son all humility, the mother
all forgiveness.—One thing, though—I haven't told her
she's a grandma. At her age it could be very dangerous.
One of these days we'll have a doctor and nurse in
attendance and break the news.—How's it all sound?
—or is it too much for your Puritan soul?

JULIEN:

Mumbling.

Thank you, Edouard—you're being very good.

EDOUARD:

No—I'm not good; you know very well I'm not. But
I like your wife and you *are* my brother. We have to
show a little family feeling once in a while. Come
along, Colombe; and stop calling me "monsieur." Try
Edouard.

They go into dressing room: COLOMBE
gazes about in admiration.

Quite something, isn't it? Ma does know how to give
things an air. Of course everything's studiously false.
Sit down on this pouf that's doing its damnedest to
look like Louis XV, and wait for me. I'll go catch the
tiger. Buck up—

38

He goes into the other dressing room.
COLOMBE *and* JULIEN *are each alone, with
a wall between them.*

JULIEN:

Suddenly.

Colombe!

COLOMBE:
Yes?

JULIEN:
You promised!

COLOMBE:

A little impatiently.

Yes, Julien. Please!

DESCHAMPS, ALEXANDRA's *co-director in the
theatre, and* POET-MINE-OWN *enter the far
end of the corridor. They are a matched
pair of top hats, frock coats, high collars,
mustaches and canes.*

DESCHAMPS:
Perfect!

MINE-OWN:
You *really* think so?

DESCHAMPS:
It's inspired.

39

MINE-OWN:
> *Fatuously.*

I must admit, I think it's quite a good new scene.

DESCHAMPS:

Poet-Mine-Own, the last act'll be a sensation.
> *Walks in front of* JULIEN.

Pardon, monsieur.
> *Recognizes him.*

Why, it's Julien. What are you doing here?

JULIEN:

Waiting for my mother.

DESCHAMPS:

> *A little uneasy.*

She knows you're here?

JULIEN:

Edouard's passed on the news.

DESCHAMPS:

Please, no fireworks just before rehearsal. We open
on the 22nd—every minute counts. Ask Robinet.
> *Notices* POET-MINE-OWN's *bristling air.*

You're not going to greet each other?

MINE-OWN:

> *Icily.*

I'm waiting.

DESCHAMPS:
For what?

MINE-OWN:
An apology.

DESCHAMPS:
Apology for what?

MINE-OWN:
Indicating JULIEN.
Monsieur knows very well for what.

DESCHAMPS:
Recollecting.
Oh—the kick in the pants! You mean that's still await-
ing settlement?

MINE-OWN:
Decidedly.

DESCHAMPS:
Julien, say you're sorry. You two can't keep on like
this. Ten to one you don't even remember what you
came to blows over.

JULIEN:
I remember perfectly.

DESCHAMPS:
You sure have changed!—Robinet, *you* show some
sense. After all, a kick in the pants isn't like a slap in
the face. A kick in the pants is no stain on the honor.

MINE-OWN:

> *Primly.*

The *seat* of the pants.

DESCHAMPS:

> *At a loss.*

Was it? Well, maybe the seat of the pants does cast a bit of a stain on the honor.—Julien, you've gotta make the first move.

JULIEN:

If I move anything, it'll be my foot. And if it's my foot, I can't guarantee *where* it will move.

DESCHAMPS:

You're really impossible. Come along, Robinet.

> *Enters the dressing room, pulling* ROBINET *—who glares at* JULIEN *and shows by the way he walks that he fears another kick— after him.—Noticing* COLOMBE.

Hello.

MINE-OWN:

> *Putting on his monocle; in happy surprise.*

Mademoiselle.

DESCHAMPS:

You're waiting for Mme. Alexandra?

COLOMBE:

Yes, monsieur.

42

MADEMOISELLE COLOMBE

MINE-OWN:

> *Flitting about* COLOMBE, *murmuring to* DESCHAMPS *loud enough for* COLOMBE *to hear.*

Exquisite, isn't she—absolutely exquisite.
> *Aloud.*

Haven't we met before, mademoiselle?

COLOMBE:

> *Rather embarrassed.*

Yes, monsieur—two years ago, at the theatre.

MINE-OWN:

> *Suddenly remembering.*

I remember now! Then you're here with—
> *Indicates* JULIEN.

COLOMBE:

Yes, monsieur. I'm his wife.

MINE-OWN:

> *In a "you'll-need-them" tone of voice.*

My very best wishes.

DESCHAMPS:

> *Who has been at the dressing room door.*

You there, Mme. Alexandra? Poet-Mine-Own is here with the new scene—it's terrific.

MINE-OWN:

> *Simpering with false modesty.*

Deschamps goes too far. But I do think you're going to like it.

43

MME. ALEXANDRA:
> *Bursting in with her retinue.*

Where's my wonderful new scene? And the little girl—very nice. Good afternoon, my dear.—Mine-Own!

MINE-OWN:

Madame Inspiration!
> *They fall into each other's arms.*

MME. ALEXANDRA:

My great, great man. When I think what a darling he is, besides being a genius.—I hope you slept well?

MINE-OWN:

I couldn't sleep. Your play!

MME. ALEXANDRA:

Oh, my play—my wonderful new scene. The Muses have drained my sweet poet. A chair, someone—a chair for Poet-Mine-Own.
> *The staff scurry about for an armchair for each of them. She stops them with a gesture.*

None for me—not today. Just a footstool—to sit at a great man's feet.

MINE-OWN:
> *Getting up.*

No, no: I won't allow it!

MME. ALEXANDRA:
What a darling. Like fresh bread. I must kiss him
again.
They kiss again.
Wonderful poet!

MINE-OWN:
Glorious artist!

MME. ALEXANDRA:
*Suddenly detaching herself: down to
earth.*
Well then—two chairs.
They sit down: she looks at COLOMBE.
Why, she's a dream! Of course her hair's all wrong.
—I'm listening, Poet-Mine-Own.

MINE-OWN:
Who has pulled a script from his pocket.
This is after the big scene—when Leonore has decided
to die.

MME. ALEXANDRA:
I see it all. She lies there, already pale as death. Her
dress is draped about her in gigantic folds—about
twenty-five yards of material.

MINE-OWN:
I'll begin:
"Moon, dear! Cold planet, lifeless as my heart..."

45

MME. ALEXANDRA:

God, how beautiful! Achingly beautiful! ... "Cold planet, lifeless as my heart!" I know just how to read it. I can give it everything.

> *While talking, she never stops looking at herself in the mirror. Suddenly, in a different voice.*

Lucien, you ass!

HAIRDRESSER:

> *Hurrying toward her.*

Mme. Alexandra?

MME. ALEXANDRA:

Just what are you trying to do to me? I look like a poodle. And what on earth are these curls? Will you please do something about it immediately! Then I want you to go to work on this young lady.—Mine-Own, I'm listening.

MINE-OWN:

"Moon, dear! Cold planet, lifeless as my heart,
Wouldst of my woes I make for thee a chart?"

MME. ALEXANDRA:

I like that better.

MINE-OWN:

> *Disconcerted.*

You don't like the first line?

46

MME. ALEXANDRA:

I mean my curls. It's very beautiful, Poet-Mine-Own
—very classical.

MINE-OWN:

"Wouldst of my woes I make for thee a chart?
Of the loved one betrayed, the loving one bereft,
Tears for the thief, curses on the theft?"

MME. ALEXANDRA:

..."curses on the theft."
Meditates.
Quite!

MINE-OWN:

"My love has the midnight, mortuary scent
Of lilies drugged with sleep. Ah, once-content,
Now bitterly unhappy heart, decide..."

MME. ALEXANDRA:

Genius, sheer genius! You see, Lucien, you've got to
quiet down my curls. And with the young lady—turn
around, dear, in the light—hair very high on the forehead, very low on the neck. Skin like velvet and she
keeps it hidden.—And who found you that mortifying
dress?

COLOMBE:

Julien, madame.

47

MME. ALEXANDRA:

That authority!—Go on, Mine-Own, I'm listening:
"Happily unbitter heart, decide!" It's already engraved
on my memory.

> *To* COLOMBE.

Darling, let me help you, you won't recognize yourself. Georgie, give me my jewel box.

MINE-OWN:

> *Continuing while* MME. ALEXANDRA *is busy
> with* COLOMBE.

"Now bitterly unhappy heart, decide
To be Life's widow—or be Lethe's bride."

MME. ALEXANDRA:

> *Getting up and patting him.*

Like ... alabaster, dear poet.—Edouard, you do have
taste.... Where did you find this pretty child?

EDOUARD:

No one would recognize her. Mother, you're a ma-
gician.

MME. ALEXANDRA:

> *Working on* COLOMBE.

Why don't you use jewelry, you little idiot—it's so
right for you.

COLOMBE:

I don't have any.

48

MME. ALEXANDRA:

I didn't either, at your age, but I used to buy things in junk shops—artificial, but better than nothing.

COLOMBE:

Julien dislikes artificial jewelry.

MME. ALEXANDRA:

Don't mention that name to me.—When people get too grand for fake stuff, they should be in a position to buy real.—Mine-Own, it's just shattering! But there's something I want to ask—you know who this child is?

MINE-OWN:

Rather coldly.

Yes.

MME. ALEXANDRA:

It's the wife Julien's saddled me with. He's joining the colors. After all the Bastille Days when I've recited the Marseillaise, you know they'd gladly get him deferred. But monsieur doesn't wish to be deferred. Monsieur is mad for military life, like his father before him. Of course he leaves his wife in Paris without a sou. She's got to have a job. Mine-Own, as long as you're doing this scene over, you could drop in something for this child. Nothing really—four or five lines, somebody who comes to console Leonore—an earth-spirit—or a sister-in-law.

49

DESCHAMPS:

> *Suddenly exploding.*

O-o-oh no! A new part that the management'll have to pay for! Not today, thank you.

MME. ALEXANDRA:

> *A thundercloud.*

Will you kindly shut up? Who are you, may I inquire?

DESCHAMPS:

I just happen to be co-director here—in charge of money matters, as I recall. Besides you're more than able to look after your own family without me. You get half the take as it is.

MME. ALEXANDRA:

Swine—utter swine! Make him leave—I can't bear having him near me.

DESCHAMPS:

We're in production. A cast of 32, and a million costumes. We won't make our expenses as it is: it's out of the question to write in another part just because...

> *Almost apoplectic.*

...blood is—tighter than water....

MME. ALEXANDRA:

All you think of is money. You sicken me. Night after night, I wear myself to the bone, I drag out my guts for your sake.

DESCHAMPS:

> *Still raging.*

When you do it free of charge I'll be delighted to thank you.

MME. ALEXANDRA:

Ho, ho, will you?

> *Suddenly wrapping herself in her dignity.*

Well—I've a sick headache coming on—I can't rehearse today.

DESCHAMPS:

> *Alarmed.*

Mme. Alexandra! We open the 22nd!

MME. ALEXANDRA:

Then we won't open the 22nd.

DESCHAMPS:

But we can't possibly postpone. Your present show won't have a leading man after the 20th—you know he's going into something else.

MME. ALEXANDRA:

We can play it without him.

DESCHAMPS:

No, we can't. Even with him, nobody comes.

> *Mastering himself.*

Mme. Alexandra, it's four o'clock. The cast has been

waiting downstairs to rehearse since half past two. We've got to open on the 22nd.

MME. ALEXANDRA *merely stares.*

Go down and rehearse—I'll do something about the girl.

MME. ALEXANDRA:
Inexorably.
Seven francs a performance—matinees, double.

DESCHAMPS:
For four lines?

MME. ALEXANDRA:
All right, she'll speak twelve lines.—You filthy trades-man, I can't think why we put up with you.

DESCHAMPS:
Licked.
All right, seven francs—even if she's invisible!—Only go downstairs now and rehearse!

MME. ALEXANDRA:
Turning toward POET-MINE-OWN.
It's a treasure of a scene.

MINE-OWN:
But I'd barely started to read it.

MME. ALEXANDRA:
That doesn't matter—I've guessed the rest. Dear friend, you will throw in a few lines for this child—she can

run through them at the end of the rehearsal. Georgie,
try to find her a dress; she can't go down there looking
like this.

DESCHAMPS:
>*Groaning.*

Please, Mme. Alexandra—they've been waiting since
half past two!

MME. ALEXANDRA:
>*Inspecting herself in front of her cheval-*
>*glass.*

Edouard, you've got a good eye—see that she looks all
right.

EDOUARD:
Yes, Mater.
>*To* COLOMBE.

Come along, Miss.

DESCHAMPS:
>*Shouting at* COLOMBE, *who doesn't move.*

Do as you're told: go try that dress on.
>*He goes out, slamming the door; passes*
>JULIEN *in the corridor without even seeing*
>*him.*

MME. ALEXANDRA:
>*In front of her mirror.*

How ducky! Now I don't look a bit like a poodle.—I
look like a seal.

HAIRDRESSER:
>*Rushing toward her.*

But Mme. Alexandra ...

MME. ALEXANDRA:
You deserve to be killed, but I haven't got time now.
—Poet-Mine-Own, Master Poet! Your scene is torrential. Only, know what I'd do if I were you?

MINE-OWN:
>*Uneasily.*

No, dear friend.

MME. ALEXANDRA:
I'd cut out the first six lines.

MINE-OWN:
But I only read you eight.

MME. ALEXANDRA:
Exactly. I'd start with the seventh:
  "My bitterly unhappy heart, decide..."
It's so much more ... instinctive that way.

MINE-OWN:
>*In despair.*

But the lilies ...

MME. ALEXANDRA:
>*Exiting the while.*

Don't let that worry you. I'll have real ones standing about in tall vases. That's better you know: always show, when you can, rather than tell.

54

MINE-OWN:

But...

> *Stunned, he exits after her. They go right past* JULIEN. MME. ALEXANDRA *either doesn't see him or doesn't want to.* MME. GEORGES *then comes out and trots over to* JULIEN.

MME. GEORGES:

It's all fixed. Mme. Alexandra was very nice—made M. Deschamps put her in the show. Mr. Edouard helped tremendously, too.

JULIEN:

> *Raising his head; stammering.*

They're p-putting her in the show?

MME. GEORGES:

Yes. M. Mine-Own is writing her a part, and she'll get seven francs a performance. You needn't worry now about going away.

JULIEN:

> *Suddenly.*

And who's going to look after the baby?

MME. GEORGES:

Oh, at his age they do nothing but sleep.

JULIEN:

> *Fed up.*

Georgie, leave me alone.—

> *Indicating dressing room.*

There's no one there now, I can go in?

MME. GEORGES:

Mr. Edouard's picking her out a dress—they want her
to rehearse this afternoon already.

Shuffling off: mumbling.

She'll get double for matinees.

EDOUARD:

Coming out, calling back.

Till tonight, princess?

Bumps into JULIEN *in the doorway.*

Have a look in. You won't recognize your wife.
Georgie tell you it's all set?—Gotta run now: will I
see you later?

JULIEN:

I doubt it.

EDOUARD:

The best of luck then, general. And don't worry about
Colombe—we'll look after her.

He goes out. JULIEN *goes into the dressing
room and stops.* COLOMBE *appears in a
charming dress, unimaginably altered. She
rushes to the mirror without even looking
at him, and squeals with pleasure.*

COLOMBE:

Julien! Don't you know me?

JULIEN:

Yes.—At least I know your voice.

56

MADEMOISELLE COLOMBE

COLOMBE:

In front of the mirror.

You can't imagine what a show they put on! They all talk at once, then they all shriek at once, then they fall into one another's arms.—Julien, they're putting me in the new show. I've got lines, I'm getting a costume. And it's nothing in the dim future—I start right in this afternoon.

Keeps looking at herself.

It's me—can you believe it, Julien?

JULIEN:

Who has closed his eyes and doesn't move. In a dull flat voice.

I don't know what to believe, Colombe.

COLOMBE *stares at herself in the mirror, no longer aware that he is there. Smiles at herself, murmurs in ecstasy.*

COLOMBE:

It's me. It *is* me.

JULIEN *turns round and looks at her.*

Curtain

Scene 2

SCENE: *A badly lighted empty stage. A tree, a table with chairs on top of it, one or two other props. Mid-stage, a work-lamp throws a skimpy light: far back, dressed up and leaning on a parasol, stands* MME. ALEXANDRA, *who barks toward the wings.*

MME. ALEXANDRA:

Well?

SCENE-SHIFTER:

    From offstage.

No one yet, Mme. Alexandra. They probably thought the rehearsal was for 2:30—the way it usually is.

MME. ALEXANDRA:

    In her noble, grand-mannered enunciation.

Crepp!

    Starts roaring and raging up and down the stage, like a caged lion.

The whoors, the 10-franc whoors. The 6-franc markdowns. The 4-franc has-beens. To keep me waiting! And they want a rrraise!—I'll give them a rrraise!

    A shadow appears timidly between two flats. It is COLOMBE *in her debut dress. She doesn't dare approach* MME. ALEXANDRA, *who, shouting "whoors" for the last time, turns and sees her. Her attitude changes as her voice does—she leans, in high-romantic style, against her parasol.*

58

Oh—it's you, dear child. I was dreaming.

COLOMBE:

I'm a little early, Mme. Alexandra—the rehearsal's not till 2:30.

MME. ALEXANDRA:

I know. But I like to come before the rest do, and be alone on the stage with the great ones who played here once, and are no more. I dream, I slip out of myself, I murmur an immortal phrase or two ... and then it's rehearsal time, and I tuck the past away.

COLOMBE:

I'm terribly sorry to have interrupted you, Mme. Alexandra. I'll go back to the dressing room.

MME. ALEXANDRA:

Oh, it's just as well—I've dreamt all I dare for one day.
         Suddenly.
You play cards?

COLOMBE:

No, Mme. Alexandra.

MME. ALEXANDRA:

That's too bad, we could have had a little game while we're waiting for those lice. I'll tell your fortune instead.

> *They take the chairs off the table, and sit in them.*

59

Here, cut the cards.

> COLOMBE *cuts*, MME. ALEXANDRA *starts laying them out.*

1, 2, 3, 4, 5—a club. That's good. Uhm . . . Still better. There's a blond young man and a nice trip somewhere. Hhm—the blond young man again.

COLOMBE:

But Julien's dark.

MME. ALEXANDRA:

Julien?—you don't suppose people have their fortunes told to hear about their husbands?

> *Lays out more cards.*

1, 2, 3, 4, 5—the king of hearts and ten of clubs together. You're going to marry a very important man with scads of money.

COLOMBE:

But I'm already married.

MME. ALEXANDRA:

That's no way to talk! I've been married eight times. Let me congratulate you, my dear.

COLOMBE:

Eight times! *Real* marriages?

MME. ALEXANDRA:

Why, I should think so—do I look half-witted? In my position, I *always* married my lovers—I even married one of them twice. Boulin—the sugar Boulin. First after his mother died, and then after his father.

60

COLOMBE:

To comfort him?

MME. ALEXANDRA:

Good God, no! To help him get going with his millions.

COLOMBE:

Were you happy with him?

MME. ALEXANDRA:

> *Looking at cards.*

The king of diamonds—another very important man for you.

> *Resuming.*

Happy with a husband who refused to bathe?—When he died, I married his son by his first wife—a nice, clean-cut boy. But the son died in my arms and what was left went back to his mother. Unfortunately, I couldn't marry her. And she knew nothing about how to handle money and died richer than any of them.

COLOMBE:

Are there really people so rich they can buy anything they want?

MME. ALEXANDRA:

No, that's the funny part. Poor Boulin—the father— would have given anything to be witty. Couldn't. He tried—all day long, wherever he went. "How do you do-do-do?" he'd say. Or "Remember me to your children—if they are yours.". . .

> *Shrugs.*

No: with all his money, he couldn't get what he wanted.

COLOMBE:

Then what do most rich people do with their money?

MME. ALEXANDRA:

They hang on to it.

> *Sees* GOURETTE *come in; screams at him.*

Oh, it's you, you clown!—Is it time for rehearsal?

GOURETTE:

No, Mme. Alexandra: rehearsal's at 2:30.

MME. ALEXANDRA:

I'm aware of that.

GOURETTE:

The concierge told me you were here, madame. I was in my office, working on your statement for *Le Matin.*

MME. ALEXANDRA:

Oh! Just what am I stating?

GOURETTE:

Your opinion of love.

MME. ALEXANDRA:

They bore me! Do I ask them for *their* opinions?

62

GOURETTE:

The editor just phoned; says that Mme. Sarah Bernhardt gave them a most vivid statement.

MME. ALEXANDRA:

> *Growling.*

I daresay.

GOURETTE:

He said it was very personal. What it came down to was, she didn't believe there *was* any such thing.

MME. ALEXANDRA:

Then say that *I* do—that I do with all my heart.

GOURETTE:

That's just what I was going to say, Mme. Alexandra. May I read it to you:

> "This tumult that has always overwhelmed us women, this imperious surge . . ."

MME. ALEXANDRA:

> *Interrupting angrily.*

You damn fool—do you want to make a laughingstock of me?

> *Cries to* POET-MINE-OWN *who has just come in.*

My other self! My second voice! Rescue me from this demented oaf. *Le Matin* wants to know what I think of love.

MINE-OWN:

> *Kissing her hands.*

What! They ask God what He thinks of God—they ask the sun its opinion of light?—Simply tell them that you *are* love.

MME. ALEXANDRA:

I can't tell them that myself. My good right hand, find me a seemly sentence or two.

MINE-OWN:

Certainly.

> *Starts.*

> Always I have given, and you have given back.
> Always you shall give, and I will give to you....

MME. ALEXANDRA:

> *Interrupting.*

Not poetry, my poet, not poetry! They know I don't write poetry.

MINE-OWN:

Uhm. Perhaps a *pensée*—an epigram.

MME. ALEXANDRA:

That's it. A nice epigram.

MINE-OWN:

> *To* GOURETTE.

Take this down. "For real love to flower, we must first root out of us the black weeds of passion."

64

GOURETTE:

A little slower, please.

MME. ALEXANDRA:

Mine-Own, what are you telling us? Love *is* passion.
My *God!*

MINE-OWN:

Yes, it . . .

MME. ALEXANDRA:

I was driven mad by love, I drove others mad.—Think
of Alfonse Sableur flinging himself, in top hat and tails,
into the lion cage at the circus. For me!
> *In a lyrical actressy tone.*

How that man loved me! He would die for me—he
would kill for me.
> *To* COLOMBE.

You're a woman—you'll understand. You love someone else, so to this man you say no—you've no choice.
—Suddenly there's a terrific roar around you—this . . .
friend has got to his feet, has leapt from the box, has
bounded into the cage among the lions. The crowds
are in a tumult, but no more than your heart, for all
at once you understand. You cry out: "Alfonse, I
love you. Come back. I am yours."—Too late!

COLOMBE:

They tore him to pieces?

MME. ALEXANDRA:

No. He got out. But then I didn't love him any more.

He should have taken me right there among the lions—
but he let the chance slip through his fingers.

MINE-OWN:

How beautiful! How womanly!
To GOURETTE.
Don't lose a word of it.—And then, dear lady?

MME. ALEXANDRA:

We left the circus in silence, my husband and I.

MINE-OWN:

And Alfonse?

MME. ALEXANDRA:

He rushed off to Monte Carlo and lost four million
francs on zero the very first night.

COLOMBE:

And then put a bullet through his brain?

MME. ALEXANDRA:

Not exactly. He married a Rothschild.

MINE-OWN:

Miriam?

MME. ALEXANDRA:

No, Hannah. The flat one.

COLOMBE:

It's like something you read in books, Mme. Alexandra. What must one be to be loved like that?

66

MME. ALEXANDRA:

Just a woman. I was soul and sex, dreaming and waking. Alfonse—and there were many like him—realized that to hold me the ordinary bourgeois attentions were not enough. He really worked at it, he made an effort. —One day, when I had no appetite whatever—I used to put my glove on my plate, actually I was trying to reduce—Alfonse, frantic that I wouldn't eat anything, made the waiter at Maxim's bring him a raw rat—and consumed it in front of me.

MINE-OWN:

How mad! How male!

COLOMBE:

And then you managed to eat a little something?

MME. ALEXANDRA:

Eat a little something? After that, I couldn't eat for weeks—ugh!—My dear, it's the perfect way to diet.
Laughing.
The best part was, Maxim's tacked 50 francs on the bill for the rat.

MINE-OWN:

Speaking of rats, I just saw our broker. Do you have any Wagons-Lits stock?

MME. ALEXANDRA:

Yes. He advised me to buy it.

MINE-OWN:

Well, he just advised me to sell it. It's due to drop.
He says to put the money into ... It's a secret, but if
we could go to your dressing room, I could hint. ...
> *She looks at him as she starts to leave the
> stage.*

There's a real killing to be made in ...
> *Lowers his voice.*

... South American copper.

GOURETTE:
> *Just as they are exiting.*

Mme. Alexandra, how shall I end your statement about
love?

MME. ALEXANDRA:

What a time to bring up that nonsense again. See me
after rehearsal.
> *Exits with* MINE-OWN.

GOURETTE:

Yes, of course. And after rehearsal—
> *Mimics.*

"Can't you see how drained out I am?" And then tomorrow, when they run Réjane's opinion of love ...

MME. GEORGES:
> *Who has tiptoed in.*

You might as well go back to your office. They're on
the subject of their investments—we'll be lucky if the
rehearsal starts by four.

GOURETTE:
>> *Muttering.*

Why the hell should I worry?
>> *Exits.*

MME. GEORGES:

We all have money problems, don't we, Mrs. Julien?
The public doesn't know. My neighbors all envy me—
"What a life you lead, Mme. Georges." You like it?

COLOMBE:
>> *Lost in reverie.*

Oh, yes.

MME. GEORGES:

You wouldn't rather be home with your husband and
child?

COLOMBE:
>> *Suddenly exclaiming.*

No!

MME. GEORGES:
>> *Looks at her, shrugs, prepares to exit.*

Well, I've got to press madame's goddess robe. Beautiful, but 95 pleats.—Oh, here's our leading man.
>> *She exits.*—GAULOIS *makes an imposing en-*
>> *trance: felt hat, flower in buttonhole, stick.*

GAULOIS:

Good afternoon, my sweet. You the first?

COLOMBE:

Mme. Alexandra's here.

GAULOIS:

Our star on time? What next?—I was hoping for a few minutes with you. How're things coming?

COLOMBE:

Mme. Alexandra says I'm doing all right.

GAULOIS:

Your progress is amazing—an awkward moment here and there, but, really, amazing. You must come to my place after rehearsal sometime, we'll go over your part.

COLOMBE:

You mean it, M. Gaulois?

GAULOIS:

A spot of sherry, a dab of pâté—we'll chat. I've a cute little place—Moroccan.
            Comes closer.
I'm mad about you. I can't sleep any more.

COLOMBE:

You ought to sleep.

GAULOIS:

I can't. I keep seeing you in front of the fire on my tiger-skin rug. I moan all night long like a condemned man. I drink and drink to forget, and I only remember. You're always there and I can never quite touch you.

70

Sometimes toward dawn I drop off exhausted—my valet finds me stretched out by the cold hearth.

COLOMBE:

Dazzled.
You have a valet?

GAULOIS:

A Moroccan.

COLOMBE:

He must be handsome.

GAULOIS:

He has a scimitar at his belt. He stands waiting with folded arms, then serves you without a word.

COLOMBE:

He's a mute?

GAULOIS:

When he should be, like all good Moroccans—and good valets. So come see for yourself. I'll put on Moroccan dress, too—a great white cloak that I got of an Arab chief. I'll squat in the corner to contemplate you.

COLOMBE:

You can contemplate me here, M. Gaulois.

GAULOIS:

No, no. I've been waiting for you all my life.

COLOMBE:

Really?

GAULOIS:

Always. And you've been waiting for me—I know you have. Has anyone else ever loved you like a condemned man?

COLOMBE:

No.

GAULOIS:

Then you've never *known* love. You've never known yourself.

COLOMBE:

But I hardly know *you*, M. Gaulois.

GAULOIS:

You know I love you.

COLOMBE:

Julien loves me too.

GAULOIS:

No doubt. But how? Would Julien roll on the ground for you?

COLOMBE:

No.

Suddenly.

Would you eat a raw rat, just to give me an appetite?

GAULOIS:

Completely thrown off.

A raw rat? Why a raw rat?

72

COLOMBE:

 I just wondered.
    Enter DESCHAMPS.

DESCHAMPS:

 Ah, Gaulois. Good afternoon.

GAULOIS:

 Good afternoon.

DESCHAMPS:

 You know, there's a costume rehearsal this afternoon.
 Alexandra's already dressed.

GAULOIS:

    Looking glumly at him and seeing through
    him.
 Well, then, Colombe, we'd better get dressed too.

DESCHAMPS:

    Countering.
 She has plenty of time; she doesn't come on till the
 last act.
    To COLOMBE.
 There's something in your contract I'd like to talk over
 with you.

GAULOIS:

 Oh, of course, the contract!—All right, see you later.
    Exits.

DESCHAMPS:

Come to my office for a minute after rehearsal. A spot of sherry, a dab of pâté, and we'll sign our little paper. I know I made a fuss the other day—but that was just for effect. Don't worry, you shall have your seven francs. Would you like some of it in advance?

COLOMBE:

Oh—could I?

DESCHAMPS:

Come in after rehearsal—and you needn't say anything to Mme. Alexandra; she counts her pennies, you know. I'm an easy mark.

COLOMBE:

Thank you, M. Deschamps. You're very kind.

DESCHAMPS:

Not with everybody. Not with everybody. Tell me— this is really your best dress?

COLOMBE:

Yes.

DESCHAMPS:

We can't have that! I know just the dressmaker who could make you just the thing—a little suit, maybe in that walnut color they're showing.

COLOMBE:

Uhm—but wouldn't you think a little fur cape with a hat to match? I saw one on the Rue de Rivoli this morning.

74

DESCHAMPS:
> *Taken aback.*

Oh!—Well, perhaps trimmed with fur.

COLOMBE:

Only what can I buy on seven francs a day?

DESCHAMPS:
> *Softly.*

We'll work it out, between the two of us.

COLOMBE:

You're terribly kind, M. Deschamps.

DESCHAMPS:

I really am, you know, in spite of my reputation.
> *Enter* POET-MINE-OWN.

MINE-OWN:

Where's my little, where's my little, where's my little nymph?

DESCHAMPS:
> *Frigidly.*

Right here. With me.

MINE-OWN:

You know, Deschamps, I can't get her out of my mind. Last night I wrote eight more lines for her.

COLOMBE:

For me?

MINE-OWN:

All for you. I couldn't sleep a wink thinking of you.

75

COLOMBE:

You, too? Nobody around here is able to sleep.

DESCHAMPS:

Robinet, you know how long the play is. You can't make it longer.

MINE-OWN:

My dear Deschamps, this child is going to be a sensation. I could give her a ten-minute monologue and the audience'd eat it up.

DESCHAMPS:

Of course: she's wonderful. But she doesn't come on till the last scene, when the women are putting on their gloves.

MINE-OWN:

For once, leave it to me. I'll work with her on her part. After the rehearsal, Colombe, you come to my apartment for a spot of sherry, and then we'll go to work.

DESCHAMPS:

She's tied up after the rehearsal.

MINE-OWN:

That's too bad; this comes first. We open the 22nd—this child has to work, Deschamps!

DESCHAMPS:

She's also got to sign her contract.

MINE-OWN:

That takes days, doesn't it? Go get it, and she'll sign it now.

DESCHAMPS:

It's being drawn up now.

MINE-OWN:

You're supposedly the businessman and you make the poet talk business. The play opens the 22nd, and this child's part can make or break it.

EDOUARD:

> *Who has come in and overheard; smiling.*

I've the solution for all of you. Since Colombe can't perform stark naked—much as we regret the fact— and there's just time enough, after rehearsal, to order her a dress, I'll take over. Her date will be with the dressmaker.

> *Smiling at them both.*

—That is, if you *really* want to open on the 22nd.

DESCHAMPS:

All right, maybe that's the best idea. See you all later.

> *Exits.*

MINE-OWN:

The theatre is a great institution, when everything else comes ahead of the script.

EDOUARD:

> *Still smiling.*

Mine-Own, Mother's looking for you.

77

MINE-OWN:
> *Unwilling to leave.*

I just this minute left her.

EDOUARD:

Since then, she's been deep in thought—and decided the new scene is too long.

MINE-OWN:

Too long? Why all she's done is cut it.

EDOUARD:

After deep thought, she only likes the very last line.

MINE-OWN:

Only one line! And what, pray, is only one line to rhyme with?

EDOUARD:

I can't tell you yet—I haven't had time to work it out.

MINE-OWN:

This is too much. Who wrote this play?

EDOUARD:

Dozens of people say you did.

MINE-OWN:
> *Like a madman.*

I'll take it off the boards. She—she can have the last line, but we'll see who has the last word!
> *Exits.*

78

COLOMBE:

This is awful. What'll they do?

EDOUARD:

Nothing whatever. This is the theatre—while they're rehearsing a drama, they're also staging a comedy.
Changing his tone.
The important thing is that I rescued you from those two old goats.
Looks at her.
Or do you find them fun?

COLOMBE:

I do in a way. They sniff, and circle round me, and roll their eyes, and say they can't sleep at night.

EDOUARD:

Who can't sleep at night?

COLOMBE:

M. Gaulois and M. Poet-Mine-Own.

EDOUARD:

Deschamps can?

COLOMBE:

Yes, Deschamps can. But he wants to give me an advance on my salary. And a little walnut-colored suit.

EDOUARD:

And what decision have you reached?

79

COLOMBE:

The suit might be very attractive.

EDOUARD:

Come, come, my sweet. Don't look so innocent. I mean, which benefactor?

COLOMBE:

There's only one. The others only offer their insomnia and a little sherry.

EDOUARD:

It's just as well I'm here to stand guard over honor.

COLOMBE:

What honor?

EDOUARD:

The family's. I'd hate to have to slap all three faces—I don't mind getting killed so much, but to have to get up three times at 5 A.M.!

COLOMBE:

You're the one with the evil thoughts: they only want to help me with my part.

EDOUARD:

They do? That's the best they could think up?

COLOMBE:

Didn't you think up the same thing? Didn't I go to your place?

EDOUARD:

Yes, but for the sake of your career. To prove it, I didn't even offer you sherry.

COLOMBE:

I noticed.

EDOUARD:

Just the script—read standing up in the dining room. It's not that I'm a moralist—but sipping sherry side by side on a divan: I don't think I could handle that.

COLOMBE:

I'm afraid I don't understand.

EDOUARD:

You don't? Well, then, my sweet: when I have fun, I have fun; and when I guard the family honor, I guard the family honor.

COLOMBE:

Since we're going to order my dress this evening and I can't come to your place, couldn't we rehearse my part now instead of talking foolishness?

EDOUARD:

Of course.
            Reaching in his pocket.
Here's my script: I'm never parted from it.

COLOMBE:

I'm sure this bores you to death.

EDOUARD:

Frightfully.

COLOMBE:

I can always ask M. Gaulois—it might not bore him.

EDOUARD:

No, perhaps it wouldn't. So *I'd* better suffer.—Let's do the end first: it wasn't right yesterday.
> *He sits—she crosses toward him.*

COLOMBE:

"And if I were to tell you I loved you?"

EDOUARD:

"I wouldn't believe it."

COLOMBE:

"And if I were to tell you I'm sick at heart?"

EDOUARD:

"With eyes like yours?"

COLOMBE:

"What do you know of my eyes—when you never look at them?"

EDOUARD:

> *Getting up and taking her in his arms.*

"Never?"

COLOMBE:

> *Lets him look at her, then turns bashfully away.*

"Not so hard, monsieur—you make me blush."

82

EDOUARD:

"You thought to play at love, and now are caught in its snare. You yearn, as much as I, for the kiss I'm about to take."

COLOMBE:

Letting her head fall on his shoulder.
"Yes, baron."

EDOUARD:

Looking at her for a moment over his shoulder, then sighing in another tone.
The baron—kisses you.

COLOMBE:

Without moving.
Was it any better than yesterday?

EDOUARD:

Yes, my angel. You little devil, where did you learn all this?

COLOMBE:

I just speak the way I feel.

EDOUARD:

Do you do it so well by imagining you're with Julien?

COLOMBE:

Julien would never talk to me like that.

EDOUARD:

Gaulois?

COLOMBE:

No.

EDOUARD:

But you still think that you're yourself—Colombe?

COLOMBE:

Yes.—A Colombe who loves the baron.

EDOUARD:

And when we do the farewell scene, you'll feel terribly unhappy?

COLOMBE:

Not really. Though I'll really want to cry.

EDOUARD:

Has Julien ever made you cry?

COLOMBE:

Yes, sometimes.

EDOUARD:

And when you cry, while you're acting, it's those tears you think of?

COLOMBE:

No. It's not the same.

EDOUARD:

But you really cry?

COLOMBE:

I cry, but I'm not really sad—deep down.
84

EDOUARD:

But when you cry with Julien—you're really sad, deep down?

COLOMBE:

Yes—that's real life.

EDOUARD:

You're sure you've never cried with him *without* being really sad, deep down?

COLOMBE:

Why do you ask that?

EDOUARD:

For my own good. I just can't believe that anyone who cries so heartbreakingly whenever she feels like it, wouldn't sometimes decide that she feels like it.

COLOMBE:

You mean I'm a liar?

EDOUARD:

What a horrible word!—But women do have their own patented way of telling the truth: only backwoods idealists like Julien wouldn't know that.

COLOMBE:

I don't like you to speak that way of Julien.

EDOUARD:

Why?

COLOMBE:

He's a real man.

EDOUARD:

I know—and women love real men. They need them
for the kind of game they play. With bad eggs like me,
they know that kind of thing won't work. But it can
still be fun.

COLOMBE:

Fun?

EDOUARD:

With people like me. You can drop the mask and
relax. It must be terribly wearing to always have to
be a womanly woman.

COLOMBE:

Breaks out laughing.
Edouard, you really *are* a bad egg.

EDOUARD:

Moving away.
Of course!—Well, shall we do the scene once more
before the high priests of art take over the stage?

COLOMBE:

If you want.
Places herself.
Suppose M. Gaulois discovers me in your arms?
86

EDOUARD:

I'm sure he would know we were only rehearsing a scene.

COLOMBE:

"And if I were to tell you I loved you?"

EDOUARD:

"I wouldn't believe it."

COLOMBE:

"And if I were to tell you I'm sick at heart?"

EDOUARD:

"With eyes like yours?"

COLOMBE:

"What do you know of my eyes—when you never look at them?"

EDOUARD:

"Never?"

> *Gets up, takes her in his arms: suddenly murmurs.*

You wicked little devil.

> *Lets her go; says with a childlike softness that cuts under his man-of-the-world air.*

Even so, we mustn't hurt Julien!

> *They stand against each other without daring to look each other's way.*

Curtain

ACT II Scene 1

SCENE: *The dressing room corridor, as in Act I,*
          Scene 1, but seen from the reverse side
          with COLOMBE's *dressing room exposed,*
          and the door to MME. ALEXANDRA's *opening*
          on the corridor. MME. GEORGES *is in a chair:*
          JULIEN, *in uniform, paces back and forth;*
          opens COLOMBE's *dressing room door.*

JULIEN:
  Is this hers?

MME. GEORGES:
  Yes.

JULIEN:
                    Closing the door.
  There was no one at the house.

MME. GEORGES:
  To come back like this without a word! We didn't
  expect you, Mr. Julien.

JULIEN:
  We suddenly got a 24-hour pass because there's a new
  general.

MME. GEORGES:
  Is the new one nicer?

  88

JULIEN:

They're all alike.

MME. GEORGES:

Now don't act the way you usually do. Tip your hat when you pass him.

JULIEN:

And be led out and shot?—She didn't even go home for dinner!

MME. GEORGES:

You know the theatre—her time's not her own.

JULIEN:

There was a woman at the house—someone she pays to watch the baby.

MME. GEORGES:

She's a very good mother—spends her last sou on the baby. You know she got a raise?

JULIEN:

A raise?
           Quickly.
Oh yes, I know!

MME. GEORGES:

Ten francs a day now. And a bigger part. I s'pose she's written you all the news here....

JULIEN:

She wrote that...

MME. GEORGES:

>*Breaking in.*

Eve and the Serpent was a flop. M. Poet-Mine-Own
and Mme. Alexandra swore and cursed at each other—
I don't know where people in their circle learn such
language. Well, then they made up and now they
have a hit—*The Realm of Passion*—the dresses take ten
minutes to hook up.

JULIEN:

And she comes on late?

MME. GEORGES:

No, she's on at the start—she'll be here any minute.
Unless Mr. Edouard took her to dinner and brings her
back in a cab.

JULIEN:

Edouard takes her to dinner?

MME. GEORGES:

Sometimes. So does M. Gaulois. That's very unusual
for a leading man. But he couldn't be nicer.

JULIEN:

I see.

MME. GEORGES:

A little thing like that who's all alone, everyone feels
sorry for her.

90

JULIEN:

I can believe it.
> *Enter* GOURETTE.

GOURETTE:
> *Shouting.*

Curtain in ten minutes!

MME. GEORGES:
> *Exiting.*

No! Madame's not here—and neither is Mrs. Julien.

GOURETTE:

That's not my lookout—I've enough to worry about.
> *Shouts.*

Curtain in ten minutes!
> *Sees* JULIEN; *changes his tone.*

Ah, Mr. Julien! This is a surprise—you managed to get off?

JULIEN:

As you see.

GOURETTE:

Army life's getting to be quite a snap. Not like in my day.—You were panting for a little theatre atmosphere?

JULIEN:

Yes.
> *After a second.*

I got your letter.

GOURETTE:

Half blushing, half sneering.

So soon?

JULIEN:

Last night. Thanks for writing.

GOURETTE:

I thought you'd want to be up on the latest stage gossip.

JULIEN:

Yes.—Got five minutes to go out for a drink?

GOURETTE:

No; it's too close to curtain time. And I have to dress—
I have to fill in, somebody got sick.

JULIEN:

Seizing him by the arm.

Then let's go in here—I'll only be a minute.

GOURETTE:

I know. But I ought to warn you, it's her dressing
room.

They go into COLOMBE's *dressing room.
A voice calls "Georgie!"*

MME. GEORGES:

Re-emerging.

Yes, M. Gaulois?

GAULOIS *appears at the entrance to his
dressing room in a Moroccan robe and his
underwear, putting on make-up.*

GAULOIS:

Would you get me my shirt?—Has our little one come?

MME. GEORGES:

Not yet. But I've a surprise—Mr. Julien has.

GAULOIS:

No!

MME. GEORGES:

I told him how nice you've been about his missus.
>   *She closes the door. In* COLOMBE's *dressing*
>   *room,* JULIEN *has been listening to them:*
>   *now he grabs* GOURETTE *by the collar.*

JULIEN:

Who is it?

GOURETTE:

That's *it!* It'd be fine if we knew right off—but that's
the tough part about having an unfaithful wife: who's
she unfaithful with?

JULIEN:

Tell me or I'll beat your brains out.

GOURETTE:

You're all alike—"I'll strangle you"; "I'll murder you."
The sure sign of the beginner! It's not that simple,
you know. It's a real part, it's one of the established
roles—the romantic lover, the heavy father, the de-
ceived husband. You've got to learn the lines, you've

93

got to know the cues. It's an art, a very great art, and it takes time.

JULIEN:

Taking him by the throat.
God damn you, cut that out—tell me, or I'll kill you.

GOURETTE:

That'd be fine training: you wouldn't even get to be an understudy.—I know: you want to prove your virility. It's useless. Stop choking me, Mr. Julien—it's not me, you can be sure of that. I'm too ugly.

JULIEN:

Letting him go, taking hold of himself.
Why did you write to me?

GOURETTE:

Because I like you—and because it made you a...colleague....

JULIEN:

You don't know who it is?

GOURETTE:

No.

JULIEN:

Who's she been going out with?

GOURETTE:

Ah, now we're getting somewhere. That's sound: a good cuckold should be methodical. I can only help

94

in small ways, you know—I'm merely the confidant.
The brilliant hunches, the inspired detective work will
have to come from you.—There are four candidates.

JULIEN:

With a start.

Four?

GOURETTE:

Four *possibilities*, that is; I didn't mean four certain-
ties. Edouard, Gaulois, Poet-Mine-Own, and our master of the revels, M. Deschamps. A lovable group,
aren't they? I think you can skip the hairdresser—
though he does do her hair an awful lot, and women
go for him.

JULIEN:

The man has a smell.

GOURETTE:

The animal in him—which you shouldn't minimize;
that could be part of his appeal. One of the first rules
of your new profession is: don't go by what *you* feel,
by any ideas *you* have in the matter. That's exactly
why most cuckolds . . . flunk.

JULIEN:

Five with the hairdresser!

GOURETTE:

Don't be upset. I knew a captain who suspected his
entire company. Think what a colonel would have to
go through.

95

JULIEN:

I'll strangle all five of them!

GOURETTE:

Yes, you can—but it won't help. You won't get relief even if the guilty one's among them.

JULIEN:

She'll be back any minute—I'll worm it out of her.

GOURETTE:

You good little boys, how you all go about it. You'll never learn *anything* that way.

JULIEN:

Groaning.
But Colombe loves me.

GOURETTE:

She may. But it won't help.

JULIEN:

I left her, like an imbecile, with this stinking gang. She's just a baby.

GOURETTE:

Uhm. The trouble with babies, we can't read their minds.

JULIEN:

What should I do?

GOURETTE:

Now you're starting to show promise. Begin by studying the classics in the field: it's going to be very strange at first, and you'll need help.—In a minute she'll come in, she'll smile, she'll kiss you: watch out, it'll all seem terribly normal. But life gets very odd for the cuckold: strange coincidences start piling up as they never used to. The letters that don't come, or come too late. The phones that ring—and there's no one at the other end. The friends you haven't seen in years who stick like a leech for a whole afternoon: all the things in ordinary life that are kind of peculiar, that you can't quite dope out—they're suddenly crystal clear! Nothing will be mysterious. The alibis will be perfect—terrifyingly perfect. There was something hearteningly ambiguous about the old life: now there's an answer for everything. Only every answer will breed ten new questions. The gas man who rings the bell won't just be the gas man—he'll be a question. The song she's humming, the article she's reading—questions. The new color of her lipstick—a tremendous question. Life will be a long weaving snake dance of questions; and you yourself will become an eavesdropping, dresser-drawer-rummaging, sounds-in-her-sleep-pondering . . . question mark.

JULIEN:

No! I'll ask her nothing.

GOURETTE:

Oh, yes, you will! And when you're all finished, you'll

have barely started. Now you'll begin on yourself—questioning yourself, doubting this, doubting that, finally deciding you invented it all. That day you will be the real thing—a *cordon bleu* among cuckolds.

> *Listens.*

Here she comes! Make up your mind, Mr. Julien: either you want help and listen to me; or you can be your own lawyer and see what happens.

JULIEN:

What shall I do?

GOURETTE:

To begin with, hide. That's another rule: always hide.

JULIEN:

> *Looking frantically around as the voices outside come nearer.*

Where?

GOURETTE:

> *Opening a cupboard and pushing him inside.*

In a cupboard—headquarters for cuckolds!

> *He has pushed him into the cupboard, now rushes out into the corridor; cries.*

On stage for Act One!

MME. ALEXANDRA:

> *Rushing in, followed by her staff.*

Stop bellowing like that, you half-wit! The curtain'll

98

go up when I'm ready.—Are you doing Doussin's part
again tonight?

GOURETTE:
Yes, Mme. Alexandra.

MME. ALEXANDRA:
Disappearing into her dressing room.
That'll be a treat for the audience.

COLOMBE:
Entering with a cry.
Where is he? Where is he?
*Goes to her dressing room, sees no one,
runs out.*
Georgie, Georgie! Where's Julien?
Goes back, sees JULIEN, *who has come out
of the cupboard, throws herself into his
arms.*
My darling! Where did you come from?

JULIEN:
The cupboard.

COLOMBE:
What were you doing in there?

JULIEN:
Playing a little joke on you.

COLOMBE:
Squeezing him tight.
This is wonderful!—It's been *so* long!

99

JULIEN:

> *Gently.*

Longer than you can imagine.

COLOMBE:

But you've been busy. All the things you had to learn, while your little friend here's been all alone, waiting for you.—This is so nice. And how handsome you look in uniform: like a general.

JULIEN:

Not yet—though there are rumors.

COLOMBE:

Sit down, I'll bet you're tired.

> *She sits on his knees.*

What's the most you have to march at one time?

JULIEN:

Twenty-five kilometers.

COLOMBE:

But they let you take a streetcar home?

JULIEN:

No.

COLOMBE:

And all the other things you have to do, your laundry and everything. I'll bet you don't have time to think of me.

JULIEN:

Plenty of time.

COLOMBE:

Of course you'd say so. But when you're not working and you're with the boys—it's a vacation, too. Good riddance to wives. If the girl back home is cold, she should take a hot-water bottle to bed.

JULIEN:

How's the baby?

COLOMBE:

Oh, he's fine.—Do you like my little walnut-colored suit?

JULIEN:

Uhm hmm—very nice. And I bet expensive.

COLOMBE:

No, not a bit. I found a dressmaker who gives you a price and lets you pay so much a week. Anyhow, you know I'm quite a money-maker now. I'll be able to treat you once in a while—so you can have fun and treat the girls. We know all about you—think we didn't know why you refused to be deferred?

JULIEN:

There are very few girls around camp, Colombe.

COLOMBE:

There are enough. I'm sure you were unfaithful.

JULIEN:

But I wasn't.

> *In a natural tone.*

And you?

COLOMBE:

Me? Darling, don't be silly: I wouldn't have even had time. I've got a pretty big part in the new play: I've had to work my head off. Are you going to come and applaud me? Knowing you're out front'll give me stage fright, but still—Oh, baby, my big sweet baby, it's wonderful to have you back. And you look so well!

JULIEN:

Do I?

COLOMBE:

> *Kisses him, stands up.*

Being without you does have its good side, it makes it so wonderful to be together again.—Will you forgive me if I dress?—We ring up any minute. I'm late.

> *She goes behind a screen. While she undresses, you see her naked arm throw a dress over the screen. Calling out.*

How long is your leave?

JULIEN:

Twenty-four hours.

COLOMBE:

Is that all? Couldn't you say you missed your train?

JULIEN:

No.

COLOMBE:

But darling, that's awful. I've been invited out after the show by some people who can do a tremendous lot for me—it would take too long to explain—and to-morrow I have to rehearse all afternoon.

JULIEN:

It's very simple—you break your date.

COLOMBE:

Oh, Julien, baby, I just can't—my whole future's involved.

JULIEN:

So is mine. And a military future can be mighty brief.

COLOMBE:

Don't talk that way.—You'll have other leaves, but I may never have another chance like this. These are very big people who could get me into the Folies-Bergères. They need somebody my type for a sketch in the next revue. Don't worry, darling, I'll wear clothing—otherwise I wouldn't even consider it.

JULIEN:

Getting up, shouting suddenly.
Stop talking such slime. Colombe, you're coming home with me tonight.

103

COLOMBE:

> *After a silence.*

It's sure like old times. You've just come back and you're screaming already!

JULIEN:

Yes, I'm screaming—and I'll scream worse if I have to. But I know this much: you're not going in for the kind of thing you're talking about.

> COLOMBE *appears in panties and corset from behind the screen.*

COLOMBE:

> *Innocently; hands across her breasts.*

What are *you* talking about?

JULIEN:

Stop playing dumb.

COLOMBE:

But I'm not, baby; really I'm not.

> GAULOIS *comes out of his dressing room, two-thirds dressed, and knocks at* CO-LOMBE's *door.*

GAULOIS:

Are you there, my little monkey? I wanted to tell you to watch your step.

> *He half opens the door, sees* JULIEN; CO-LOMBE *has run behind the screen.*

Oh, forgive me.

JULIEN:
  Forgive *me*.

GAULOIS:
  Enjoying your leave?

JULIEN:
  Immensely.

GAULOIS:
  Good!—You know the new scene?

COLOMBE:
  Yes, M. Gaulois.

GAULOIS:
  Good! We're using it tonight.
> *Goes back to his dressing room.*

JULIEN:
  Why does he call you his little monkey?

COLOMBE:
> *Emerging.*
  I don't know. He's got a nickname for everybody.
  —He's helped me a lot with my part.
> *Now* DESCHAMPS *rushes around self-impor-*
> *tantly; taps discreetly on* COLOMBE'*s door.*

DESCHAMPS:
  Are you there, my little titmouse?

JULIEN:
  Now it's a titmouse.

DESCHAMPS:

I just wanted to tell you to watch your step.

Has opened the door—sees JULIEN.

Oh!—sorry.

JULIEN:

So sorry.

DESCHAMPS:

Awfully sorry. I wanted to tell your wife something.
—Everything all right?

JULIEN:

Everything's all right.

DESCHAMPS:

You look fine.

JULIEN:

Thanks. That's what everyone says.

DESCHAMPS:

To COLOMBE *behind the screen.*

I wanted to tell you we're going up on time tonight!
Don't be late.

He trots off.

JULIEN:

Little titmouse. From that scum. God, he's awful.

COLOMBE:

Emerging.

There you go. You have to see the worst in everything.

106

They shouldn't think of me as a little monkey, they shouldn't think of me as a little titmouse: what *do* you want them to call me—*"Madame la duchesse"?*

JULIEN:
How could you make friends with such scum?

COLOMBE:
I haven't made friends with them. I see them every day—I have to work with them. Nobody else is so disagreeable about nothing the way you are. Anyhow, they amuse me.

JULIEN:
Don't say that: they can't.

COLOMBE:
Why can't they?

JULIEN:
Because I know you too well.

COLOMBE:
> *With a cool look.*

You think so?

JULIEN:
Yes. And in the end you'll go back to being yourself, whether you want to or not.

COLOMBE:
> *Facing him with the look of an enemy.*

My poor Julien.

MME. GEORGES:
> *Tiptoeing in.*
Glad to see one another?

JULIEN:
Tickled to death.

MME. GEORGES:
It's nice to come back to a wife that everybody raves about, but who's just for you.
> *Hands* COLOMBE *her petticoat.*
Look at that little figure, Mr. Julien—you could eat her up. And what a hit she's made. M. Mine-Own thinks it's his play that's packing 'em in, but we know otherwise. Aren't you happy to have such a big success of a wife?

JULIEN:
I could puke from joy.
> POET-MINE-OWN *appears in the corridor: knocks discreetly on* COLOMBE's *door.*

MINE-OWN:
Are you there, my little turtle-dove?

JULIEN:
> *Tiptoeing to the door; bellowing.*
Yes, I'm here!

MINE-OWN:
> *Jumping at man's voice.*

Forgive me—do please forgive me.—I just wanted to tell you to watch your step.
>*Stops.*

Forget it, it's nothing—I don't know what I'm saying, I'm so nervous—the King of Spain's out front. Act your best tonight, dear little lady—and do forgive me.
>*Trots away.*

JULIEN:

Now it's a turtle-dove. What is this: Aesop's fables? How could you let that slimy old character call you his turtle-dove: I told you never to speak to him.

COLOMBE:

But he wrote the play I'm in.

JULIEN:

Isn't it enough to have to speak his *lines?*—And why do they all want you to watch your step? Count of me—hhm?

COLOMBE:

Can't you ever let up?

JULIEN:

And you smile at them, and purr at them. . . . Wipe off your mouth: I can't stand the way you look.

MME. GEORGES:
>*Stopping him.*

Mr. Julien, you'll ruin her make-up. It's her job right now to smile. Look at her—crying. Imagine what'll happen if it drips on her mascara!

JULIEN:

Georgie, get out.

MME. GEORGES:

Not if you're going to make her cry!

JULIEN:

Taking her arm and putting her out.

When I say get out—you get out.

JULIEN comes back. MME. GEORGES starts to walk off, then walks back, puts her ear to the door and gradually, during the scene, the HAIRDRESSER, CHIROPODIST, GOURETTE in Louis XV costume, and most of the cast silently collect in the corridor behind COLOMBE's door.

JULIEN:

Suddenly.

Who is he?

COLOMBE:

Who is what?

JULIEN:

Your lover.

COLOMBE:

Please, Julien, stop it. I haven't got a lover.

JULIEN:

Grabs her: wildly.

You tell me who it is!

COLOMBE:

Darling, how can I tell you something I don't know?

JULIEN:

It's no use, Colombe: I've got proof. Somebody saw you—and wrote and told me.

COLOMBE:

Freeing herself: furious.
Who dared to write you?

JULIEN:

See—you're scared. No use pretending; I've a letter on me giving the whole story.
Mimics the others.
... My little snake.

COLOMBE:

I want to know who wrote you.

JULIEN:

I'm sure you do.

COLOMBE:

An anonymous letter no doubt. They all hate you in this business, they're all jealous. Go on, act like a detective, now that you've started all this: ask the janitor, ask the old man who walks the dogs, ask the old woman who mops up the men's room—you'll hear plenty of stories. I won't have one lover, I'll have twenty. They're only happy spreading filth. Anonymous letters while they sit around waiting for parts they'll never get. You'd think you'd know better after being raised in this atmosphere. But you'd rather believe *them* than show a little confidence in your own wife. They don't even have to sign their names.

Changes her tone: close to tears.

Those two glorious years when we were broke and I cooked and cleaned and did everything I could to make you happy—*then* you never questioned my fidelity. Do you think this is the first time men have paid attention to me? Do you think if I'd wanted to be unfaithful I had to wait for you to go in the army?—It never once entered my head, even when we went without dinner and pretended we'd just come back stuffed from Maxim's. Go on, forget all that, just roll me around in the mud.

She falls sobbing on a chair. JULIEN *doesn't move.*

JULIEN:

I'm sorry.

COLOMBE:

You're sorry—you're sorry! It's done now. You'd believe anyone rather than me.

JULIEN:

I want to believe you.

COLOMBE:

In a low colorless voice. From beneath her tears.

The letter was signed?

112

JULIEN:
  Yes.

COLOMBE:
  Tell me her name.

JULIEN:
  It was a man.

COLOMBE:
  Thinks for a minute: exclaims.
  Oh, now I see! It would never occur to you that this
  ... pig wrote the letter out of spite, because I wouldn't
  agree to his charming proposals?

JULIEN:
  Leaping up.
  Who wanted you to?—Tell me his name!

COLOMBE:
  No—you tell me, so I can see whether he's the one.
  Let me just guess the first letter. It's a P, isn't it?

JULIEN:
  No.

COLOMBE:
  O—oh! An R! *That's* who it is—that disgusting crea-
  ture!

JULIEN:
  No—it's not a P *or* an R.

COLOMBE:

It's not a W? Low as he is, I don't think, because a woman refused him, he'd do a thing like this!

JULIEN:

No, Colombe, it's not a W.

COLOMBE:

No. But if he's not the one ...

JULIEN:

What do you mean—if *he's* not the one?

COLOMBE:

My poor Julien, I can't even guess who it was—there's been one after another. They try to follow you into your dressing room, and you have to slam the door. They grab hold of you in the corridor and you have to slap their face. What do you think happens to a halfway attractive girl when men know she's alone?

JULIEN:

Shouting.

I want their names—I want every one of their names!

COLOMBE:

My poor darling, you'd need the telephone book. Men are men—don't act so surprised, I'm sure you're no different.

JULIEN:

Since I met you, I've never looked at another girl.

COLOMBE:

Oh, of course not—you wouldn't dream of it.—What about the Chenaud twins, when you were teaching them waltzes for four hands.

JULIEN:

They were fifteen years old!

COLOMBE:

Precisely. The dark one wasn't much, I admit—but the other, with her silly child-like manner and firm mature breasts. You were always leaning over to show her the right position for the fourth finger. I dare you to deny it—I've received letters, too, in my day—only I didn't say anything.

JULIEN:

The Chenaud kids—it's insane.

COLOMBE:

And the druggist's wife?

JULIEN:

The druggist's wife?

COLOMBE:

Yes, my pet, the druggist's wife. You'd never go on an errand except when we needed tooth powder or soap—and when we were broke that tightwad, who'd skim milk at both ends if she could, would give *you* credit!—I'll give you credit, too—you had quite a

way with her.—And to ... to say these things to me
—I'm not joking, Julien, I think you're awful.

> *She starts to cry a second time.* JULIEN
> *stands silent, at a loss for what to do: in
> the corridor, they feel that things may be
> straightening out and something had better
> be done. With pantomime, they persuade
> the* HAIRDRESSER *to go in. He knocks and
> half opens the door.*

HAIRDRESSER:

They're going to ring up, madame. Shall I run the
comb through your hair once or twice?

COLOMBE:

> *In tears.*

Oh thanks, Lucien—yes, I need it.

> JULIEN *begins getting suspicious again
> when the* HAIRDRESSER *comes in: looks
> them over suspiciously while* LUCIEN *works
> on* COLOMBE.

COLOMBE:

> *Smiling into the mirror.*

You're a nice man, Lucien—you try to make women
pretty.

HAIRDRESSER:

> *With an embarrassed smile toward* JULIEN.

You're always pretty to begin with. Doing your hair's
not work, it's a pleasure.

116

JULIEN:

See here, my friend!

> HAIRDRESSER *turns around, comb in mid-air.*

How long does it take to "run the comb through her hair once or twice"?

HAIRDRESSER:

It depends, Mr. Julien.

JULIEN:

Depends on what?—And the comb's not enough; it also requires your hands, I see.

HAIRDRESSER:

You can't comb *curls.*

JULIEN:

Get out of here—or I'll run more than a comb... through more than your hair.

> *Pushes him out. Comes back, shouts.*

He's not the one.

COLOMBE:

He?

JULIEN:

He couldn't be your lover. His hands are like dough. How can you let him touch you? Answer me, Colombe, before I start a scene: it's not him?

COLOMBE:

> *Getting up with a cry.*

I know who wrote to you! It's not true when you say it's a man. All these hysterics because a drunken old bat saw me having dinner with the hairdresser.

JULIEN:

Springing up.
You had dinner with him?

COLOMBE:

I do have to eat, you know. Am I supposed to fast because you're in the army?

> *In the corridor the* HAIRDRESSER *is very much annoyed: the others make fun of him.*

JULIEN:

That baboon had the nerve to ask you to dinner—and you actually went? I'll—beat his brains out.

> *Runs toward the door: the* HAIRDRESSSER *pushes through the crowd away from the door.* COLOMBE *catches hold of* JULIEN.

COLOMBE:

Darling, you're behaving like a child. He's a greasy half-wit who never opens his mouth. Do you think if I wanted a lover I'd pick anything like that? Show a little sense!

JULIEN:

He's *not* very pretty, is he?

COLOMBE:

> *Laughs, kisses him.*

118

My great big dope of a husband! I have him do my hair because he's so good at it: but otherwise—really I prefer you.

Takes his hands, kisses him again.

Instead of fighting with me ever since you came, couldn't you once take me in your arms?

She melts into his arms, locks his hands behind her, offers her lips.

JULIEN:

Weakly.

But who is it then?

COLOMBE:

It's no one, you dope. No, there is somebody—I'd better fess up. It's you.

She kisses him.

JULIEN:

In her arms.

I love you, darling, and I'm so miserable. It'd be better to tell me if you've done something wrong. Don't you think I know how tough it is to be all alone? And in this filthy atmosphere. I'll get you out of it and we'll be happy again.

COLOMBE:

Caressing him: genuinely tender.

My sweet foolish baby, who frightens everybody and is more defenseless than all the others—you're a brave man just the same.

JULIEN:

Groaning, while she caresses him.

But how could you let them come near you—that fool that calls you his little monkey—

COLOMBE:

Gaulois?

Guffaws in the corridor.

Fool is right! He thinks he's irresistible because he was good-looking 30 years ago. So he mumbles and whispers and tries to look passionate—

GAULOIS *hurries into his dressing room.*

JULIEN:

And you let him—

COLOMBE:

Yes, I let him . . . talk. That's all he *can* do. "My little monkey," and "my little mousie," and "I can't sleep for love," and "I can't eat for love"—and I'm sure he can't love for love, either. Pats your hand and then hurries home exhausted and takes off his corset and drinks his cocoa and sinks into bed. And he's in raptures because he has the strength to get up by noon the next day—and strap on, and lace on, and buckle on, and hammer on, all his orthopedic appliances—and come back here and try to hold hands with one of the other girls. You think I need *that*—when I have you?

JULIEN:

But what did he mumble and whisper about?

COLOMBE:

Well—that I should rehearse with him at his apartment
—all done up in what he calls Moroccan style.

JULIEN:

And you went?

COLOMBE:

Upset.
No, darling—Yes, I did go: but not alone. With Poet-
Mine-Own, to run through a scene.

JULIEN:

You see, the letter I got was true. You do go around
with them, you do go to their apartments....

COLOMBE:

But I told you: I went with Poet-Mine-Own, in his
carriage.

JULIEN:

Wounded once more; shouting.
But then you were alone with *him!*

COLOMBE:

Trying to be patient.
But I took him along so I wouldn't be alone with
Gaulois.—Really, Julien, I couldn't bring someone else
along so I wouldn't be alone with *him.*

JULIEN:

Remember how Mine-Own behaved two years ago:
I had to teach him manners.

COLOMBE:

You were a very good teacher! Now he's courtly, but
very well-behaved.

JULIEN:

Courtly: and you let him be: you let him pay you
court. M. Robinet of the Academy—a man like that
has juicy little parts to hand out. So we let him kiss
the back of our glove—and then stroke the back of
our arm—and then ... it's really very little, consider-
ing what you'll get out of it. Too bad he has a tic;
but you can stand it, can't you? Well, I can't! I've a
little courting to do, too, with that old—

> Starts wildly for the door. Consternation
> in the corridor. COLOMBE grabs him, while
> breaking into laughter.

COLOMBE:

Darling—this is insane. Really it is!

JULIEN:

What's so funny?—Because I'm ashamed? Because I'm
upset?

COLOMBE:

No, no! What you say—that he has a tic. Can you
imagine me in the arms of Poet-Mine-Own? Julien—
just think of him in his underdrawers!

122

She starts to laugh again: slowly her laughter wins him over.

JULIEN:

I must admit that Mine-Own in underdrawers would be quite a sight!

COLOMBE:

Laughing more.

You don't know the best part of it! He wears baby-pink garters that his wife embroidered.

For a moment they both roar with laughter; suddenly they both stop.

JULIEN:

How would you know?

COLOMBE:

Regaining her laugh.

Everyone does.

JULIEN:

How do *you* know?

COLOMBE:

Deschamps told me.

JULIEN:

Deschamps? That's the kind of thing you discuss with Deschamps! When was this?

COLOMBE:

If you let me, I'll explain.

JULIEN:

Don't tell me you went to his office—sat on the green divan where he gets reimbursed for handing out parts?

COLOMBE:

No—well yes, once. Please let me explain, Julien: when I signed my contract.
>   *After a second.*
All right, if you *must* know. He didn't make me any exception to what he does. I stopped him—I slapped his face. I told him what I thought he behaved like—and what I thought he looked like, too. Then I s'pose for fear Poet-Mine-Own might have a little better luck, he told me what *he* looked like—garters, and a few other details. Darling, that's all there was to it!

JULIEN:

>   *Suddenly slapping her face: shouts.*
Just a tramp, like all the rest. God damn you!
>   COLOMBE *falls down in a faint:* JULIEN
>   *rushes toward the door.* MME. ALEXANDRA,
>   *dressed as a maréchale, who had come out
>   of her dressing room to listen with the
>   others, pushes them all aside; and when*
>   JULIEN *opens the door, she stands directly
>   in front of him:* MME. GEORGES *glides into
>   the dressing room to look after* COLOMBE.

MME. ALEXANDRA:

>   *In her most terrible voice.*
Well, sir?

JULIEN:
Let me through—I want to see—

MME. ALEXANDRA:
>   *Blocking him.*

Must you mess things up wherever you go? Do you
always have to scream and start trouble? I felt sorry
for you and took in your wife: now you get out of
here and leave us alone.

JULIEN:
It's you...
>   *To the crowd.*

... it's you who did this to her.
>   *To his mother.*

And you, looking like a—I can't say what you remind
me of. God damn you all!

MME. ALEXANDRA:
>   *Like thunder.*

Stop that! I'm your mother.

JULIEN:
Yes, you're my mother. Who'd know better than I?

MME. ALEXANDRA:
You think I care for it? If it's not money, it's scenes.
You let this child alone—she was just beginning to
enjoy herself. Is she supposed to lock herself up for
life because you had the good taste to fall in love with

her? Women will stick—if there's something to stick
to!

> *To* GOURETTE.

Ring up! And get that child on stage dead or alive!
The audience is already making a commotion on ac-
count of this fool!

> *She exits grandly, her cane tapping in
> rhythm. Having parted to let her pass, the
> others follow, while* GOURETTE *shouts.*

GOURETTE:

On stage for Act One! On stage for Act One!

> *At this* COLOMBE *miraculously revives:
> looks in the mirror.*

COLOMBE:

Is my hair all right?

MME. GEORGES:

It's fine, dear. Come along, I'll put your dress on
downstairs.

> *Everyone has gone except* JULIEN *who
> goes, half drugged, into the deserted
> dressing room. Below, the three taps are
> heard and the orchestra begins the over-
> ture to* The Realm of Passion. *After a min-
> ute* EDOUARD *appears—walking jauntily in
> time with the music and carrying a tiny
> bouquet. He goes into* COLOMBE's *dressing
> room, stops in surprise on seeing* JULIEN

and doesn't know what to do with the bouquet.

JULIEN:

Looks at him: suddenly in a stunned tone.
It's you.

EDOUARD:
It's me all right.

JULIEN:

This time in a sad voice.
It's you—I know it's you.

EDOUARD:

Looking quizzical.
Sorry—I don't guess I know the combination.
Nervously.
—I'd have thought you'd be glad to see me. You look fine.

JULIEN:
Yes—I look fine.

EDOUARD:
Army life not too hard?

JULIEN:
Damn hard.

EDOUARD:

Still trying to be casual.

Your feet holding out? When they go, everything goes.

> *Tries to laugh, but stops, seeing* JULIEN's *face.*

JULIEN:
You're feeling chipper?

EDOUARD:

> *Suddenly very much upset.*

No.

> *For a moment they stand silent, face to face.*

JULIEN:
Why did it have to be you?

EDOUARD:

> *Quietly, after a moment.*

What can you expect? You know what it's like around here.

JULIEN:

> *Shouting.*

No, I don't know what it's like—I'll never know what it's like!

EDOUARD:

> *Lowering his head.*

No, I guess you won't. You're different: you always were; even as a kid, you fought against it. I couldn't, even as a kid—when it only meant chocolates. It's never stopped—I'm scum.

JULIEN:
  Yes.

EDOUARD:

What are you going to do?
                JULIEN *doesn't move. Loudly.*
Hit me . . . hard—hurt me. I want you to. You ought
to have done it oftener when we were kids.

JULIEN:
                Choked.
No, not you—I can't hurt you. I just want to know
why. I can't understand.

EDOUARD:

How can you understand our kind of life? We're not
for you. All these slimy little male and female games
—you'd never understand, if you lived to be a hun-
dred. Sock me, hard as you can: that's so much
simpler—we'd be two little boys again.—I can't **ever**
say no, but this time I realized I'd have to get what was
coming to me—I even want to get it.

JULIEN:
  No. I can't.

EDOUARD:
                Suddenly.
The little slut.

JULIEN:
                Hollowly.
  Quit that.

EDOUARD:

You think she acted right? I'm not defending myself, I'm damn weak. But she—she knew how you loved her....

JULIEN:

Making a terrible effort.
God damn you, stop that!

EDOUARD:

She had you, she had something—solid. And the first guy that fussed over her a little—he didn't even have to try hard.—You're lucky, to be above all this.

JULIEN:

Yes. Just look at me.

EDOUARD:

I can't—I'm too ashamed.

JULIEN:

Suddenly.
I said to look at me.

EDOUARD:

Turning away.
Sock me if you want—but I can't.

JULIEN:

Forcing him.
I said look at me!
EDOUARD *raises his eyes.*

130

What's it all about?—a good enough nose, but what the hell? A pretty little girl's weak mouth. The eyes of a drunk—the look of a baby-faced dissipated old man.

EDOUARD:

You think I'm proud of it?—But you live off in space somewhere, you don't know what life is.

JULIEN:

I'm beginning to find out.

EDOUARD:

Trying to regain his poise.

You'd do better to go back to camp and forget about us all. At bottom you really want a hard life—something you can feel resentful about.

JULIEN:

You're not even very clever with those cheap pearls of wisdom you pick up in club bars. I don't think you've ever been really moved in your life.

EDOUARD:

That's not so. I've got just as much heart as you have. Only . . .

JULIEN:

Only it's still wrapped in tissue paper in the box it came in.—If you'd had an air about you—but you even dress like a . . . jockey.

Loudly.

Why? In Christ's name, why?

EDOUARD:

Exactly. *You* dope women out!

JULIEN:

I've got to find out. I've got to know what Colombe...
... Kiss me.

EDOUARD:

Embracing him, tears coming to his eyes.
You mean it—you mean you'll forgive me?

JULIEN:

Harshly holding on to him.
Not that kind of kiss—the kind you gave *her!*

EDOUARD:

Trying to break away.
Have you gone crazy? For God's sake, let me go.

JULIEN:

Struggling with him.
Kiss me. Exactly the way you did her. I've got to
know what she saw in you.

EDOUARD:

Struggling.
My God, Julien—you're losing your mind. Let me go!

JULIEN:

Catching him by the throat.
Kiss me, you stinking lousy bastard, the way you did
her!

EDOUARD:

> *Choking.*

You're choking me.—Julien, I can't.

JULIEN:

You could, once. Go on, pretend it's her.

> *He holds* EDOUARD *against himself.*

EDOUARD:

> *Struggling again.*

I can't.

> JULIEN *pushes him brutally away.* EDOUARD *gasping, falls into a chair.* JULIEN *doesn't move: looks around with a tormented face.*

JULIEN:

> *In a voice of despair.*

Colombe: I don't understand.

Fast Curtain

Scene 2

Curtain goes up on the final scene of The Realm of Passion. *Louis XV décor as conceived around 1900. A salon with French windows opening onto a terrace: beyond, a Watteau-like park.*

On stage at rise: MME. ALEXANDRA *and* GAULOIS.

MME. ALEXANDRA:

Too long my lips were sealed, my heart on fire.
Now come, sweet youth, come swooning to my arms.
I am, like you, nineteen; I whisper, "Yes."

GAULOIS:

High lady, is it you?

MME. ALEXANDRA:

'Tis I, indeed.
My young love opens to the fragrant night:
Erst I have never dared: tonight is elsewise!
Long in a golden cage my heart has paced
On fire but frustrate: now it melts the bars,
The fire mounts and Love is himself aflame!

GAULOIS:

My star!

MME. ALEXANDRA:

With a gesture of receding modesty.
And now blot out my exalted rank!

134

Tonight no grande dame, but the maiden clay
Your hand shall mold, the white and quivering flesh
Your flesh shall warm! Yours only, yours to take.

GAULOIS:

> *Getting up with much personal difficulty,*
> *and pressing himself madly against her.*

Mine, mine forever, forever sweetly mine!

MME. ALEXANDRA:

Moments there are millenniums cannot match!

GAULOIS:

For your body's rapture, I thank you on my knees.

MME. ALEXANDRA:

> *Suddenly crying out.*

Quick, off your knees, sweet boy! Quick for he comes!

> GOURETTE *appears, playing the Maréchal*
> *de Villardiers.* COLOMBE *has come in, terri-*
> *fied, through another door, and stations*
> *herself humbly near* MME. ALEXANDRA.

GOURETTE:

Oh hateful sight! Oh heinous treachery!
Monsieur de Bouglaire kneeling at her feet!

MME. ALEXANDRA:

> *Like a Racine heroine.*

Monsieur the Marshal of France, I love this boy!

135

GOURETTE:

> *Grand and terrible.*

Wrath such as mine could cost your swain his life!

GAULOIS:

Yours to decree, M. the Marshal of France!

GOURETTE:

> *With a smile at once noble, wistful and profligate.*

I envy this boy's youth, I crave his ardor—
My royal master does not wish the sword
A Marshal wears to avenge such injury:
Our swords, monsieur, must serve a nobler cause:
Post have I all night sped here from Versailles:
War is declared!

GAULOIS:

> *Drawing himself erect, hand on sword.*

War, sir?

GOURETTE:

Gallantry,
My gallant, moves from a lady's couch
To the river Rhine, to save our glorious France!

GAULOIS:

> *Drawing his sword; piously.*

Dear France!

> *Trumpet-calls in the distance.*

GOURETTE:

Yes—one name we can both adore
With never a thought of doing each other hurt.

Turns to MME. ALEXANDRA.

Oh chide him not, Marie, if France he choose—
She is the fiercer mistress—but our Mother!

MME. ALEXANDRA:

Heartbroken but excessively noble.

Go, both of you, and leave me to my tears:
So fair a rival I too must wish should win.

GOURETTE:

Becoming very human.

I know how so you suffer: I too have loved.
Loved *you*, Madame!—Alas! Adieu!

To GAULOIS.

Monsieur!

GAULOIS:

With a helpless gesture, to MME. ALEXANDRA.

Adieu!

Amid a blare of trumpets, he follows
GOURETTE *out;* MME. ALEXANDRA *falls sobbing into* COLOMBE's *arms.*

MME. ALEXANDRA:

My gallant boy!

COLOMBE:

Trying to console her.

He will return, madame, still faithful to you!

137

MME. ALEXANDRA:

After a brief reverie.

He—yes! But I?

COLOMBE:

You?

MME. ALEXANDRA:

I am young and fair:
Others will come tonight to pay me court—
And madness 'twere, to make Love bide the morrow:
Women will die for love—but not sit waiting!

Sounds of a minuet in the park.

Clorinda, let us dance! Come, let's away:
The fiddles sing their love songs by the fountains;
Masked figures haunt the shrubbery. Come, sweet
child:
I'm nineteen—I'm a woman—I'm bewitched!
Come, let us blend the violet with the rose,
And swooning in Love's arms, forget Love's woes!

*While music is heard offstage and there is
dancing far upstage, they exit as fast as*
MME. ALEXANDRA'*s robes will permit.*

Curtain

*Frantic applause. Curtain is raised; every-
one takes bows.* MME. ALEXANDRA *and*
GAULOIS *are recalled several times; she
yielding the stage to him, then coming on
alone to be cheered. She receives flowers;*

MADEMOISELLE COLOMBE

is choked with gratitude, indicates how grateful she is to the rest of the cast; then the curtain comes down for good. At once everybody's attitude changes: MME. ALEXANDRA *tosses her flowers to* MME. GEORGES, *who has hurried over with* MME. ALEXANDRA's *cane. She exits, worn out.* GAULOIS *follows, taking off his wig while exiting.*

GAULOIS:

God, they were a tough crowd tonight.
Still in costume, but without his hat and sword, GOURETTE *helps the stagehands start to clear the stage.* JULIEN *comes on and stops* COLOMBE. *During their scene together, the lights go out and the stagehands clear the stage, till the two of them are left alone in semi-darkness.*

JULIEN:

I've been walking the streets all evening—I've got to talk to you.

COLOMBE:

Moving a little.
I have to go up and undress.

JULIEN:

Blocking her.
Not, not up there. I can't face them any more: I'm too ashamed.

COLOMBE:

All right, we'll stay here.

JULIEN:

I've seen Edouard.

COLOMBE:

Without expression.

Yes.

JULIEN:

He told me. You've seen him, too?

COLOMBE:

Yes.

JULIEN:

You realize it was all the harder to take because it was him.

COLOMBE:

In a composed little voice.

Of course I do. I'm terribly sorry. We'd both have given anything to spare you this.

JULIEN:

Ever since we were kids, he's taken things from me; he can't help it. And now—you're *both* young and pleasure-loving, and I left you here alone. And I realize that I lectured you too much, I got on your nerves, I guess.

COLOMBE:
Yes.

JULIEN:
The whole time I was walking the streets, I kept talking to you out loud. I explained everything to you. People stared at me, they probably thought I was crazy. I'd bump into them and say "Sorry" and walk on. Funny how you can walk and smile and keep saying "Sorry" when all the time you're dead.
Silence.
You know, being dead makes you a lot easier on people. I want to forgive you, I really do: only first I want to understand.
COLOMBE *has listened patiently; suddenly she speaks in a very calm way.*

COLOMBE:
It would take a terribly long time to explain. And I'm petrified I'll be late. Don't you want to come up to my dressing room so we can talk while I get dressed?

JULIEN:
Loudly.
Late? Late for what?

COLOMBE:
Quietly.
For the supper date I told you about.

JULIEN:

Not wanting to believe her.

After what's happened, you don't mean you're going to keep your date? I go back to camp tomorrow.

COLOMBE:

I told you what it can mean to my future.

JULIEN:

Are you out of your mind?

COLOMBE:

It's you who won't understand. Why do we have to stay here—we could talk just as well upstairs. They'll be calling for me any minute.

JULIEN:

Brutally turning her around.

Look at me! Even now you're acting. You're pretending not to care so you won't have to face up to what you're doing.

COLOMBE:

No, I'm not. I'm willing to answer anything you want to ask. All I want is to dress at the same time because I'm scared I'll be late.

JULIEN:

After all that's happened between us, you're able to leave me and go out and laugh with a bunch of strangers!

142

COLOMBE:

I'm not going with them to laugh. I told you why I'm going. I'm thinking of my future.

JULIEN:

Your future! It's quite different from your past: if we fought in the old days, you were always very sweet to me afterwards.

COLOMBE:

I want to be sweet now: I understand. But you ought to understand, too.

JULIEN:

It's just not possible. You can't have stopped loving me.

COLOMBE:

Who says I've stopped loving you?

JULIEN:

This thing between us is going to fester. We've got to stop it right away. You've been foolish, but we've still an awful lot to fall back on.

> *After a moment, almost with shame.*

We have the baby.

COLOMBE:

> *Annoyed.*

I was waiting for you to bring that up.

JULIEN:

Wasn't it natural?

COLOMBE:

Sure. It's very easy for you to get sentimental about the baby. But he's my baby too, and I love him very much. And right now someone I'm paying with what I make is looking after him. And tomorrow morning it'll be me who wakes him up and bathes him and dries him off and gets his breakfast. That's what he's interested in, not what goes on between us. When he's older, I'll tell him how unhappy you made me, and that one day I couldn't take it any more.

JULIEN:

I made you unhappy?

COLOMBE:

Yes.

JULIEN:

But I did everything I knew how.

COLOMBE:

Yes, everything you liked. You liked to stay home, so we never went out. I was so young and unsure about everything and you carefully explained what was right and what was wrong, so I used to say yes. But I really wanted to go dancing.

JULIEN:

We *went* dancing.

COLOMBE:

Twice in two years. And if anyone else asked me to dance, you made me refuse.

JULIEN:

But you said you loved me—

COLOMBE:

Couldn't I love you and also want to go dancing?

JULIEN:

I never dreamt you wanted to!

COLOMBE:

Of course you didn't! You thought I'd much rather stay home and hear your lectures on morality and how stupid people can be—or you played Beethoven by the hour, when if even for a minute I listened to a street singer with a guitar, you'd hurry over and slam down the window.

JULIEN:

But I wanted you to like what was . . . beautiful.

COLOMBE:

Who were you to decide what was beautiful? Things are beautiful if you love them, and I loved gypsy music and dancing and pretty clothes. But you never tried to find out what I might want, never asked me anything, never bought me anything.

JULIEN:

We hadn't any money.

COLOMBE:

And you couldn't be bothered to make any. All that mattered was your becoming a great pianist. And so that you could become a great pianist, I had to wash dishes and scrub floors. And if you'd ever become one, while you stood bowing and drinking in the applause, I'd have had my beautiful red hands to show the public.

JULIEN:

Please don't—this is awful.

COLOMBE:

It *is* awful. But it's over. I support myself now, I live the way I like. When something amuses me I laugh without worrying whether you'll think it's funny, or start to sulk as soon as we get home.

JULIEN:

If I sulked it was because it hurt me to see you suddenly do the kind of things that . . .

COLOMBE:

Well, I won't hurt you after this. We've both suffered plenty from your always being hurt. It's good to be sensitive but really, Julien, there are limits. Would you like me to be honest? I've been very happy since you

146

went away. When I wake up the sun's shining, I look out the window and for the first time in years there's no tragedy in the street. And if the mailman rings and I go to the door in my nightgown—there's no drama. I'm not a loose woman—we're just a young girl and the mailman, happy with each other—he because he gets a kick out of seeing me in a nightgown, I because I've given him a little pleasure. I like the whole business—being attractive and nibbling breakfast while I do the housework, and washing myself in the kitchen, naked, with the window open. And if the old man opposite runs for his opera glasses, I can't get excited, or feel I'm a loose woman and cry for two hours trying to calm you down. You'll never know, my darling, how uncomplicated life can be—without you.

JULIEN:

But if I was jealous and made scenes, it was because I loved you. So would any other man.

COLOMBE:

No. Or if he does, I'll have sense enough now to laugh.

JULIEN:

Edouard doesn't love you—you know he doesn't.

COLOMBE:

I know he doesn't love me the way one dreams of being loved. But he makes me happy and that's a lot. He tells me I'm beautiful and brings me little presents and takes care of me.

JULIEN:

Me! Me! That's all you know how to say.

COLOMBE:

Yes, I've learned. I heard the word often enough from you.

JULIEN:

I'm hurt.

COLOMBE:

It's very sad. But I was hurt, too.

JULIEN:

But I never meant to hurt you—whatever I did, it was because I loved you.

COLOMBE:

No, Julien—because you loved yourself.

JULIEN:

That's nonsense.

COLOMBE:

The girl you loved was something you dreamt up. I want the next man to love *me* and I want loving me to make him happy. It never made you happy. You'll never understand women—but that's all they know how to do in the world—make men happy. You shouldn't cheat them out of it.—Now I'll be late. We've said everything: let me go and get ready.

JULIEN:

Grabbing her by the wrist.

No.

COLOMBE:

Let me go.

JULIEN:

No.

COLOMBE:

You're hurting me, Julien.—Go ahead, you know how. Slap my face. It won't be the first time tonight.

While they've been speaking, the props and furniture have been removed, leaving only the sofa they have fallen onto while struggling. The stagehands come up to them.

STAGEHAND:

Mr. Julien, we've got to move this, too.

JULIEN gets up without a word; the men take the divan. JULIEN has drawn COLOMBE to him. They're alone and face to face, on a big empty stage lighted only by a work lamp.

JULIEN:

We're crazy to yell at each other. I'm going to talk to you very quietly: will you listen?

149

COLOMBE:

No.

JULIEN:

Grabbing her wrist.
You're going to have to!

COLOMBE:

You're stronger than I am: you can even kill me if you feel like it. The poor wronged husband—I'm sure they'd acquit you.

JULIEN:

I only want to ask one thing. Will you promise to answer?

COLOMBE:

It all depends. What is it?

JULIEN:

When I came into your dressing room a while ago, why did you throw your arms around me?

COLOMBE:

Because I was so glad to see you. I mean it.

JULIEN:

And then when I questioned you, when I suspected the others, why did you deny it as though you'd never even kissed another man?

150

COLOMBE:

Imagine being suspicious of those characters!—But I'd never have admitted it about anybody. It could only make things worse. I love you; you have to go back to camp tomorrow. This was no time to upset you.

JULIEN:

Why did you take my hands and kiss them and put them around your neck?

COLOMBE:

So you'd believe me—I wanted you to be happy.

JULIEN:

And if I hadn't seen Edouard, and *had* believed you? You'd have come back from this supper date and got into bed with me?

COLOMBE:

Yes.

JULIEN:

And given yourself to me?

COLOMBE:

In a small even voice.

Of course.

JULIEN:

After a silence.

I don't understand.

151

COLOMBE:

You never understand anything! I love you—that's all. You're all alone in camp. You've just spent three months without a woman—I know you haven't been unfaithful. If you hadn't found out, do you think I'd have invented a headache or something to spoil your leave? I'm not that mean.

JULIEN:

And you'd have gone through with it like a street-walker, without any pleasure?

COLOMBE:

Sincerely.

Why without any pleasure? You give me a lot of pleasure.

JULIEN:

And Edouard?

COLOMBE:

Yes. But that's something else. You have a real genius for complicating everything.

JULIEN:

And you'd have told him about it?

COLOMBE:

Indignant.

Of course not! What business is it of his? Edouard hasn't any rights over me. Look, I've never let him say one word against you. What do you think I am?

Silence. JULIEN, *stunned, dares not answer.*

152

COLOMBE:

Softly.

Baby, you'll let me go and get dressed now? I promise I won't stay at Maxim's long: I'll come home to you as fast as I can.

JULIEN:

As though questioning himself.

We really still love each other—at any rate, this way?

COLOMBE:

Yes.

JULIEN:

I'm ashamed to ask—you never just pretended with me?

COLOMBE:

No. Never.

JULIEN:

Then why? I just can't understand why.—Do you love Edouard more than me?

COLOMBE:

No.

JULIEN:

As much?

COLOMBE:

Do you think I keep score? Could I go out with Edouard all the time, let him look after me, and then give him a kiss on the forehead and say, "Run along now." *You've* got to make a little effort to understand, too.

JULIEN:

Unhappily.

I do—I don't do anything else.

COLOMBE:

But *our* way—not just yours.

JULIEN:

Then, if this leave hadn't turned up, you'd have gone on sharing the two of us?

COLOMBE:

If.... If. I don't live on *ifs.* *If* you'd stayed in Paris, this would never have happened. But you didn't: it's partly your fault. Don't always blame other people.

JULIEN:

I had to go into service sometime, like everyone else.

COLOMBE:

If you'd loved me, you could have got deferred. They said they could get you, and you refused. That's precisely when I realized that you think of no one but yourself and that I'd better start thinking of myself, too.

JULIEN:

Suddenly tender.

My poor baby.

COLOMBE:

Yes, your poor baby. And you're not making her look any prettier when she needs to!

JULIEN:

My poor little baby—all she can think of is her supper date!—I loved you the way a little boy loves his mother, or loves another little boy when they prick each other's blood and swear eternal friendship. The way two people do who plan and struggle and worry together till they're old and, sitting side by side, start dreaming back. To love that way seemed all the romance a man could need: he could forget about the things he'd never done; forget about the girls you *don't* forget about.

COLOMBE:

A little hurt.

Now you can do them—and take the girls along. Ask them to go away with you, as you did me two years ago.

JULIEN:

Yes, I could.

COLOMBE:

I can see you bewitching them with your sad eyes and your beautiful wounded soul.—What a little nitwit I was!

155

JULIEN:

> *Grabbing her wrist; loudly.*

Don't run down the old Colombe; at least *she's* still mine.

COLOMBE:

Yours, my poor dodo? What did you know about her? You thought she was a little angel?—in a florist shop where a bunch of old bucks came day after day for their carnations? And the funeral wreaths I'd take to grief-stricken households: but there was always a cousin who'd manage to control his grief and push you in a corner. Keep your little angel if it makes you happy: but there aren't any angels. Even if you want to be...

JULIEN:

> *Grabbing her.*

Damn you, I won't let you throw mud at that girl!

COLOMBE:

> *In an I-will-if-I-feel-like-it tone.*

It's me, after all!

JULIEN:

No—it's not you!

> *Looks at her with both pity and hate.*

That's what scares me worst of all—that you could get to be so vile I'd stop loving you.

COLOMBE:

Quietly.

You're hurting me, Julien—in a minute I'll be all black and blue. I can't see where that'll do us any good.

JULIEN:

Suddenly letting her go.

All right—this time you can go. Hurry up, keep your date.

She turns and walks off without looking at him as soon as he has released her. He watches her go; suddenly cries.

JULIEN:

Colombe!

COLOMBE:

Turning.

Now what?

JULIEN:

Tormentedly.

Nothing.....If while you're dressing you decide to break your date, I'll be waiting here.

With a slight shrug, she turns and exits. JULIEN *remains alone, disconsolate, in the middle of the stage. As he stands there,* MME. ALEXANDRA *appears bundled up in scarves and leaning on a cane: after her comes* MME. GEORGES.

157

JULIEN:

Mother!

MME. ALEXANDRA:

What do you mean—"mother"? Have you gone crazy?

JULIEN:

Mother, I'm so unhappy.

MME. ALEXANDRA:

You made your bed—now you'll have to lie in it alone.

JULIEN:

Mother, I loved her—I'll always love her.

MME. ALEXANDRA:

Your father would have always loved me. That's what made everything so impossible. What *is* this mania to love someone all one's life? Why should we? Do we always wear the same clothes? Do we always live in the same house? Ask the doctor, he'll tell you that there's not a cell in your body that was there seven years before. Everything else about us changes—why shouldn't our feelings change? These romantic ideas you people pick up in books—they've nothing to do with life. If your sensitive colonel of a father had started in the way I did, in a mangy old road company at fourteen, he'd never have committed suicide.—Let's go, Georgie. You haven't forgotten my knee pad?

JULIEN:

Clinging to her.

But all the same you must have suffered. Nobody can reach your age and not suffer. There must be something we can say to each other: I feel so desperately lonely.

MME. ALEXANDRA:

You'll always feel lonely. Always—because you never think of anyone but yourself. You think *I'm* the selfish one? The really selfish people aren't those who insist on having good times. They're not dangerous, they don't take any more than they give. They know only too well: they pass one another by, they pat one another's hand, you say hello to me, I say hello to you: we both know how little it means, but we can both put up a little better with what's gnawing inside us, what no one gives a damn about except ourselves. The dangerous ones are those who stop you every time you want to turn around, who instead of patting your hand, insist that you feel their guts. And the more they suffer, the more they make you suffer, the happier they are.

JULIEN:

Groaning.

But I love her!

MME. ALEXANDRA:

Yes, I guess that's true. But now she doesn't love you any more. That's just as true, that counts just as much.

What's she supposed to do—be bored to death for the next sixty years because that's the one way to keep you happy?

JULIEN:

I did everything I knew how....

MME. ALEXANDRA:

Yes, but you didn't *know* how—and you never will. Go home and go to bed and tomorrow go back to being a soldier. Spill those guts of yours for France: she may thank you for them; we can't.

> *Wincing with pain.*

Let's go, Georgie—my knee's killing me from standing here.

> *She hobbles toward the wings. Suddenly calling out.*

Was it money you wanted?

JULIEN:

No, Mother—thank you.

MME. ALEXANDRA:

Have it your own way.—Try to get some sense!

> *She and* MME. GEORGES *exit.* JULIEN *is alone on the empty stage. Goes to the piano, opens it, plays a few notes of a song, stops. We hear far off a girl's voice singing the song. "Colombe," says* JULIEN, *"do you remember?—I remember." Lights dim till it is dark.*

When the lights slowly come on again for the EPILOGUE, JULIEN *is in civilian clothes, and about to play the same piano. The stage is still empty and only lit by a work lamp, but sunlight streams through the air shafts. Then* COLOMBE *stands there in an old dress, carrying a large florist's basket of flowers. She seems to have lost her bearings; suddenly catches sight of* JULIEN.

COLOMBE:

I'm sorry, monsieur: Mme. Alexandra's dressing room?

JULIEN:

It's up a flight. But why don't you wait here?—she'll be down any minute to rehearse. That'll save you a whole flight of steps and a tornado. She's all set to blow down the theatre.

COLOMBE:

Is something wrong?

JULIEN:

In the theatre, something's always wrong.

COLOMBE:

She's such a wonderful actress—and isn't she beautiful?

JULIEN:

Oh, very. Like an old public building. Do you go for the Louvre?

COLOMBE:

That's mean of you. And she's not old: I saw her act once.

JULIEN:

That's different. On the stage she looks 20.

COLOMBE:

That's not very nice, seeing you work for her. What if she heard you?

JULIEN:

Still at the piano.
She has. I'm her son.

COLOMBE:

You're her son?

JULIEN:

Uh hum. Not that either one of us boasts about it.

COLOMBE:

Then, you see, she isn't old.

JULIEN:

Smiling, and turning round on the piano stool.
Why?

COLOMBE:

Stammering a little.
Because you're ... so very young.

162

JULIEN:

Blushing, and stammering, too.
I don't go in much for compliments—but you're ter-
ribly pretty.
A sudden pained silence between them.
Is it fun to be a florist?

COLOMBE:

Not always as much as it is today.

JULIEN:

You must meet a lot of people.

COLOMBE:

Yes, only it's mostly *old men* who buy flowers.

JULIEN:

When I'm rich I'll buy some—and give them to you.

COLOMBE:

Really?

JULIEN:

Do people ever give you flowers?

COLOMBE:

Never!

JULIEN:

What about your boy friend?

COLOMBE:

I don't have one.

JULIEN:

Suddenly getting up and coming to clip a
rose from the basket.

Here—I'll start in right now.

COLOMBE:

Oh, the basket! This'll cause trouble.

JULIEN:

I'll take care of it. There'll be trouble anyhow, just because I'm here.

COLOMBE:

Smelling her rose.

Funny, when they're given to you, you feel like smelling them. Doesn't your mother like you to come to the theatre?

JULIEN:

No.

COLOMBE:

She's afraid you'll meet the wrong type of people?

JULIEN:

Laughing.

That's marvelous! No: she's afraid I'll ask her for money. I'm trying to be a concert pianist and I practice eight hours a day: that doesn't leave much time to earn

164

a living. So sometimes I have to come here for...
supplies. As seldom as possible, because I hate the idea.

COLOMBE:

It's good to have pride.

JULIEN:

It's also tough.

COLOMBE:

If I loved somebody, I'd want him to have pride—to
be a real man.

> *They smile but don't know what to say
> next.*

JULIEN:

Do you make lots of money as a florist?

COLOMBE:

Oh, with tips about 100 francs a month.

JULIEN:

Then you're in my class.—If ... if I pick you up after
work some night, would you have dinner with me?—
you wouldn't insist on Larue?

COLOMBE:

I wouldn't even know where it was. But I once had
dinner at Poccardi's.

JULIEN:

Well, we'll go there again.

COLOMBE:

And eat up all the hors d'oeuvres?

JULIEN:

Sure, and then yell for more.

COLOMBE:

You really *will?*

JULIEN:

I hereby *do*. Tonight. Why wait?

COLOMBE:

You can't call for me tonight; this was my last errand.

JULIEN:

Gets up and takes her hand.
Wonderful: then we can start off right now.

COLOMBE:

But there's my basket.

JULIEN:

Just leave it here. It's big enough—they're sure to notice it.

COLOMBE:

Suddenly practical.
Do you think I should wait for my tip?
166

JULIEN:

I'm crazy: we both gotta wait for our tip. We'd sure do well at Poccardi's on my 21 sous.

COLOMBE:

I suppose you think I always say yes—like this. But it's really the first time.

JULIEN:

It's the first time I ever asked anyone.—Do you think it's possible?

COLOMBE:

What?

JULIEN:

That people can like each other—no, it's not just *like* —can feel something about each other right away?

COLOMBE:

I don't know.

JULIEN:

Who has sat down next to her on a bench, and puts his arm over her shoulder.
Do *you* feel that way?

COLOMBE:

Yes.

JULIEN:

Do you, very often?

COLOMBE:

No.

JULIEN:

I *never* have. I'd better tell you before we go out—I'm a dreadful person. I don't like people, I get infuriated at them—and they don't like me.

COLOMBE:

I don't believe it.

JULIEN:

It's true, though.

COLOMBE:

You seem very nice to me.

JULIEN:

You know—I find that I can be!—Ever go to the zoo?

COLOMBE:

Um hum.

JULIEN:

D'you ever watch the bears? I'm a bear. Think you'd like to tame me?

COLOMBE:

Leaning against his shoulder.
They're strong. They protect you—and keep you warm. There's nothing wrong with bears.

JULIEN:

Maybe not, but most girls don't like them.

COLOMBE:

I'm not sure what I like; but right now I know I feel fine. The only thing that scares me is—it's all happening so fast.

JULIEN:

I'm even more scared than you are. I've waited all my life for a girl who likes bears.

COLOMBE:

I'm glad.

JULIEN:

If it were only true—if it could be like in fairy tales: at first sight, and then forevermore. Promise me you'll be faithful till tonight at any rate—till Poccardi's.

COLOMBE:

I promise.

JULIEN:

Cross your heart.

COLOMBE:
>*Doing so.*

Cross my heart.

JULIEN:
>*Shyly.*

Is it too soon to kiss you?

COLOMBE:
>*Whispering.*

No.

>*Offers him her lips. He kisses her, then suddenly stands up and cries out.*

JULIEN:

God, this is wonderful!—Can life really be good? Is mother really charming and young, after all? We've got to celebrate this.
>*Takes the basket.*

Here, why be stingy—take the rest.

COLOMBE:
>*Worried.*

But they were sent to your mother, monsieur.
>*Suddenly.*

Monsieur what?

JULIEN:

Julien. And you?

COLOMBE:
Colombe.

JULIEN:
Mademoiselle Colombe! But what is happening tonight that makes life suddenly seem so wonderful?

> MME. ALEXANDRA *rushes in, followed by her staff:* MINE-OWN, DESCHAMPS, GOURETTE.

MME. ALEXANDRA:
Slime! Those bit-part players are all slime! And we open in three days.

> *Sees* JULIEN *and stops.*

What are you doing here? You're all we need!

JULIEN:
Mother darling, as you see, I'm kissing the florist.

MME. ALEXANDRA:

> *Not understanding.*

What are you talking about? Mademoiselle, put the flowers down; Gourette, give her ten sous. And Deschamps, could you have the kindness to arrange for a few auditions this evening?

DESCHAMPS:
But the little brunette who tried out this afternoon—

MME. ALEXANDRA:

The little brunette is chiefly able to wiggle.

MINE-OWN:

Who has been looking at COLOMBE.
But we're all crazy—for two hours we've been wrangling . . . over a girl to play a little florist—and here we have one! And an enchanting one!

MME. ALEXANDRA:

Inspecting her.
She *is* nice. Turn around, dear—let me see your legs.

COLOMBE:

Flabbergasted.
My legs?

MME. ALEXANDRA:

You've never heard of legs before?

MINE-OWN:

Come, little lady, show us your legs: they may make you famous.
He lifts her skirts.
They're adorable—see for yourselves.

COLOMBE:

Pulling down her skirt.
But, monsieur—

MINE-OWN:
  A bit higher, just a tiny bit higher.

JULIEN:
          Coming forward and pulling down CO-
    LOMBE'*s skirts.*
  That will do! You leave this young lady alone!

MINE-OWN:
  But we've got to see her legs—they're part of the plot.

JULIEN:
  They're always part of the plot.

MME. ALEXANDRA:
  That will do, Julien.
              To the others.
  I agree she has pretty legs. But she still needs to have
  a voice.

DESCHAMPS:
  Ever done anything in the theatre?

COLOMBE:
  No, monsieur, I work in a flower shop.

MME. ALEXANDRA:
  Have you ever done any singing?

COLOMBE:
For my own pleasure.

MME. ALEXANDRA:
Do you know "Love Is Gone"?

COLOMBE:
Sort of.

MME. ALEXANDRA:
We'll see. Julien!—where is that oaf?

JULIEN:

From his corner.
I'm here.

MME. ALEXANDRA:
Go to the piano and accompany this girl.

JULIEN:

Without moving.
No.

MME. ALEXANDRA:
What do you mean, no?

JULIEN:
I've a badly infected finger.

MME. ALEXANDRA:
Where's it infected?

JULIEN:
It's *getting* infected.

MME. ALEXANDRA:
You're a real honest-to-God little stinker. Why won't you play?

JULIEN:
Because I'm not in the mood. Because I think you should leave this girl alone. She's happy where she is.

MME. ALEXANDRA:
> *To* COLOMBE.

Sing without any piano.
> *To* EDOUARD, *who has just come in.*

Edouard, can you play "Love Is Gone" with one finger?

EDOUARD:
I can play Haydn's *Creation* with one finger.

MME. ALEXANDRA:
Then accompany this child: Your brother has refused to.

EDOUARD:
All right, let her rip.
> *Starts to play.*

COLOMBE:

Singing.

A leaf in the spring
  Will cling to the tree,
A leaf in the fall
  Will blow away.

So love like the leaf
  Will cling to your heart,
  Will sing at the start
And then will vanish.

But life must still go on....

MINE-OWN, *in rapture, after hovering over
her, puts his arm around her waist. She
tries, while singing, to free herself.* JULIEN
suddenly strides over and pulls MINE-OWN
away from COLOMBE.

JULIEN:
  You stay away from her.

MINE-OWN:
  Who put you in charge?

JULIEN:
  This young lady is *with* me.

MME. ALEXANDRA:
You don't even belong here yourself!

JULIEN:
This young lady is with me.

MME. ALEXANDRA:
That will be your exit line! Etienne! Jacques!

STAGEHANDS:
Yes, Mme. Alexandra?

MME. ALEXANDRA:
Escort this clown to the street.

STAGEHANDS:
Go on, Mr. Julien. Say bye-bye.

JULIEN:
Keep your hands off me.
They try to push him out; he fights them.

STAGEHAND:
Get going, Mr. Julien.—Hey!

COLOMBE:
Terrified.
Stop that. Make them stop, they'll hurt him.
JULIEN *has managed to get out of their clutches and starts running around the stage.*

177

JULIEN:

> *Yelling.*

Besides, before I leave, I've a duty to perform.

> *Goes up to* MINE-OWN, *turns him around and kicks him in the pants.*

I swing an adorable leg, too!

DESCHAMPS:

> *Yelling at the same time.*

Get him out of here!

> *The* STAGEHANDS *have taken hold of* JULIEN *and are starting to drag him out.*

MME. ALEXANDRA:

I'm leaving myself.—The girl's all right, I'll settle for her. Georgie, try to find her something to wear—we'll rehearse her after dinner.

MINE-OWN:

> *Hurrying over to* COLOMBE.

It means fame, my child.

> *Whispers in her ear.*

I'm wild about you.

JULIEN:

> *Yelling as he is dragged off.*

Let me go, you bastards!

> *To* COLOMBE.

Poccardi's? You said you would!

COLOMBE:

> *Pulling away from* MINE-OWN.

You're disgusting—all of you.

> *To the* STAGEHANDS.

Let him alone.

> *To* JULIEN.

I meant it! I'll go with you to Poccardi's.

MME. ALEXANDRA:

What's all this crepp about Poccardi's? You've got a job. You rehearse tonight!

COLOMBE:

Yes. But before I got the job, I accepted an invitation to dinner.

MME. ALEXANDRA:

Oh? Indeed!

> *Turning abruptly to* DESCHAMPS.

Go fetch your little brunette—if she's free for the evening. At least she won't act like Joan of Arc.

> *Exits.*

DESCHAMPS:

Thank you, dear lady. You'll see—she's most unusual.

> *Exit.*

MINE-OWN:

> *Starting to exit, then halting as* JULIEN
> *returns.*

Monsieur, two of my friends will wait upon you to-morrow.

JULIEN:
Splendid. Though I fear they won't find me at home.
Puts his arm around COLOMBE.
We're both ... vanishing tonight.

MINE-OWN:
In a rage to COLOMBE.
You ridiculous little fool.
Exits as fast as dignity permits: JULIEN *wants to go after him but* COLOMBE *prevents him.*

COLOMBE:
Tenderly.
No.

JULIEN:
Did you hear what he said?

COLOMBE:
No, I'm too happy. I heard something much nicer.

EDOUARD:
Who has stayed at the piano: smiling.
Well, my lovebirds, that was quite a scene—you sure know how to bring down the curtain.—Have you known each other long?

180

JULIEN:
  An hour.

COLOMBE:
  Don't tell him what happened—he won't believe it.

EDOUARD:
  You'd rather go to dinner at Poccardi's with this...
  crank than get started in the theatre?
            To JULIEN.
  Where did you find such a marvel?

JULIEN:
  That's my secret.

EDOUARD:
  No, don't tell.
            To JULIEN.
  I hope you're not planning to make her miserable—
  you're not going to deliver your famous series of
  lectures?

JULIEN:
  No.

EDOUARD:
  Be happy, my children!—And say, I had good luck for
  once last night—we'll go halves like brothers.

JULIEN:
            Taking the money.
  You're terribly kind, Edouard.

EDOUARD:

>*About to exit.*

Have fun! Have as much fun as you can!

COLOMBE:

Thank you, monsieur.

>*He goes out. They come back to each other.*

JULIEN:

Here we are.—I'll always remember what you just did.

COLOMBE:

You mustn't feel that way—I didn't even know I was doing it. I screamed, didn't I, when they started to put you out—and then I found myself in your arms. It's happened too fast, hasn't it—it can't be the real thing.

JULIEN:

Terribly fast, but I think it *is* the real thing—and for the rest of our lives.

>*They kiss: she leans against him, murmurs.*

COLOMBE:

My darling. The rest of our lives.

JULIEN:

That's the very least. . . .

COLOMBE:

Pressing hard against him.

Always....

More softly.

Always, always....

They kiss.

JULIEN:

Now the story begins!

They walk off happily, arms around each other's back.

Curtain